AMERICAN VIBES

People, Places and Perspectives

Todd Rucynski
Yoko Nakagawa
Videos by Todd Rucynski

KINSEIDO

Kinseido Publishing Co., Ltd.
3-21 Kanda Jimbo-cho, Chiyoda-ku,
Tokyo 101-0051, Japan

First published 2020 by Kinseido Publishing Co., Ltd.

Design   Nampoosha Co., Ltd.
Video production   Todd Rucynski

Photo credits
@TRUCZYNSKI (except the following images)
p. 9 ©photosbymeem.com (Oswego), p. 14 ©Tupungato|Dreamstime.com, p. 15 ©Eg004713|Dreamstime.com,
p. 20 ©Jim Roberts|Dreamstime.com, p. 21 ©9and3quarters|Dreamstime.com (left),
©Og-vision|Dreamstime.com (right), p. 23 ©Irinabozkaya|Dreamstime.com (lower left),
p. 26 ©Victor Moussa|Dreamstime.com, p. 27 ©Iofoto|Dreamstime.com,
p. 33 ©Alena Redchanka|Dreamstime.com, p. 38 ©Arienne Davey|Dreamstime.com,
p. 39 ©Joe Sohm|Dreamstime.com, p. 44 ©Jacqueline Nix|Dreamstime.com,
p. 45 ©Paul Morgan|Dreamstime.com, p. 51 ©Meinzahn|Dreamstime.com,
p. 53 ©photosbymeem.com (upper right), p. 54 ©photosbymeem.com (1),
p. 56 ©Bratty1206|Dreamstime.com, p. 60 ©Reinout Van Wagtendonk|Dreamstime.com (2),
p. 62 ©Kit1nyc|Dreamstime.com, p. 63 ©Linda Williams|Dreamstime.com,
p. 68 ©Typhoonski|Dreamstime.com, p. 75 ©Valentin Tulea|Dreamstime.com,
p. 80 ©Tupungato|Dreamstime.com, p. 81 ©Erik Lattwein|Dreamstime.com,
p. 86 ©Nightbox|Dreamstime.com, p. 87 ©Jason P Ross|Dreamstime.com,
p. 92 ©Juan Moyano|Dreamstime.com, p. 93 ©Trekandshoot|Dreamstime.com,
p. 95 ©Juliengroundin|Dreamstime.com (upper right), ©Aaron Wells|Dreamstime.com (lower left),
p. 98 ©Kelly Vandellen|Dreamstime.com, p. 99 ©F11photo|Dreamstime.com

🎧 音声ファイル無料ダウンロード

https://www.kinsei-do.co.jp/download/4094

この教科書で 🎧 DL 00 の表示がある箇所の音声は、上記 URL または QR コードにて
無料でダウンロードできます。自習用音声としてご活用ください。

▶ PC からのダウンロードをお勧めします。スマートフォンなどでダウンロードされる場合は、
　ダウンロード前に「解凍アプリ」をインストールしてください。
▶ URL は、**検索ボックスではなくアドレスバー（URL 表示欄）に入力**してください。
▶ お使いのネットワーク環境によっては、ダウンロードできない場合があります。

🔘 CD 00　左記の表示がある箇所の音声は、教室用 CD（Class Audio CD）に収録されています。

Preface

Language is culture. The two cannot be taught or learned apart from one another. The best way to learn a language is to travel to a country where the target language is spoken and experience the culture. As this is not always possible, learning from interesting content is the next best thing. *American Vibes* is our answer to those who are interested in learning English through American culture. This textbook is meant to take you on a journey where you will learn, not only the language and history, but what lies in the hearts and minds of Americans.

It is impossible to capture how Americans think about any one topic. It is a diverse country with passionate people who love to share their opinions. We interviewed over 70 people from age 15 to 100, so learners can get a true picture of how Americans think and feel about a variety of issues. As a teacher, it was important for me to find real people using natural language to discuss things that they truly care about. It is also important that, because this book is video-based, you can see the non-verbal ways people communicate. This is a feature rarely found in textbooks today.

As for traveling around and finding interesting cultural and historical things to present; there is no better job. I was able to combine two things I care deeply about. The first is teaching English to Japanese students — something I have done for the last 25 years. Next is trying to present the fascinating country, where I was born and raised, as a fun and interesting topic of study. The result was a true combination of depth and humor that I hope the students will find as captivating as I did.

Our journey was intense: two years, 20,000 kilometers, 11 different states or districts, and over 60 on-location reports capturing the images of America and the thoughts of those people. Looking back, it was the best job in the world. What could be better than meeting new people and learning new things every day? It was an absolute pleasure and I hope that feeling comes through when you use this book on your journey of English learning.

Todd Rucynski

Acknowledgments

First, I need to thank the fabulous crew of Fluent Films. We had Jack Lee III as production manager on the East Coast, Sarah Moliski in California, and the indefatigable Mikuko Nagashima, in-between, filling more roles than I could possibly mention. Your passion and energy fueled this project. Script supervising, additional camerawork, as well as other production duties were performed by Michael Harter, Itsuka Homma, Daniel Wiseman, Kanako Arimoto, Kevin Brown, Yu Matsuoka, Mizuki Kudo, Quinn Otterbeck, Shione Niinuma, Seth Schroeder, and Taiga Rucynski. This never would have happened without your valuable contributions.

All drone footage and photos filmed by Meem Andrisakis. You can see more of his magnificent work here: https://www.photosbymeem.com/

Big thanks to Tom McCaffrey for the perfect song: "Lake Ontario Twilight" by Frostbit Blue ©

Make up for Sarah Moliski @sarahmoliski provided by the fabulous @alethea_spencer in LA.

Of course, this book is nothing without the people who generously shared their voices and ideas:

Boston: Rich from http://www.caseysdiner.com/, Sandra, Hana, Coach Scott and the Bunker Hill Community College Soccer Team. Maine: Chrissy, Mike, and Ben from https://www.lukeslobster.com/ New York City: Isaac, Yobi, Alexandra, Jerry C., Alex, and Jeffrey. Washington, D.C.: John, Evlondo, Ashley, Mary, Sam, and Josh. Charleston: Zach, Brendan, and James Scott of http://jamesmscott.com/ Savannah: James Byrne and Marvin. Oswego: Banna, Eve, Gwen, Dom, Tom, Mike, Jack, Jason and Carol from http://rudyshot.com/ Austin: Clinton, Erika, Ariel, and Alehandro. Saint Jo: Randy, Donna, Mike Karnes at Custom Boots, Carrie and Alan & Denise Chamberlain at the Four Winds Ranch. Santa Fe: Kata, Andres, Hector, Sofia, David, and Georgina. Arizona: Colton, Mercedez, Shawn, Brian, and Clementine. Los Angeles: Jay Mohr, Sarah, Lauryn, Alethea, Sergio, Carl, and Aya. Seattle: Maddie, Quinn, Daniel, and Steve.

Special thanks to my friend Jay Mohr for giving his time, support, and apartment, and for being the first Hollywood star in a Japanese textbook. Study more at: https://www.jaymohr.com/

Please have a look at the art of Donna at https://donnahowellsickles.com/ and Randy at http://randymeador.com/. I will always remember real Texas hospitality. Thank you both.

Invaluable insight and editing were provided by Timothy Gutierrez (readings) and Jun Iesaka (voices). I consider you both brothers. My sanity has been saved by both of you more than once.

Last but not least, the team from Kinseido. Big thanks to Michi Tsutahara for enduring my time schedule. I know that wasn't easy. I am grateful that you pushed me when I needed to be pushed. Thank you to my new writing partner, Yoko Nakagawa. I am sure your Japanese contributions will greatly enhance the appreciation of our content by both students and teachers. Finally, to Aoi Nishida, an editor who never misses a thing, and a wonderful human who knows exactly how to handle me under pressure. Thank you for always making our books the best they can be.

Chapter Overview

Warm-up

Answer these simple questions in order to activate what you know about the topic. Think about what you already know about a place or issue.

Vocabulary Preview

Learn or review these words and expressions that you will meet in the videos.

 ### Part 1 Getting to Know the Place

Watch the first video to learn about the city in the chapter. You will also hear from people who live there. Answer the questions to check your understanding of what you learned from the video.

 ### Part 2 Learning More

Watch the second video to go a little deeper into the city and the historical, cultural and/or social issues which affect the city. Some chapters also feature local people who talk about their views on the place. Develop your note-taking skills through completing the cloze exercises following the transcript of the video.

 ### Reading

Read a short essay on historical events or social issues relevant to the city. Gain a deeper understanding of the area and the successes and challenges people living there have faced. Answer the questions to test your understanding. Start a discussion based on the issues raised by the questions. The reading section is followed by **American Eyes**, a Japanese column that taps into historical and cultural topics of interest adjacent to the chapter.

American Voices

Listen to Americans who share their thoughts and opinions on a variety of issues. The English is authentic as they are not actors. Practice speaking about the issues before you watch. Listen closely, then expand your ideas by adding words and expressions that you hear the people use. React to the people's viewpoints; expand your ideas and express yourselves better than before. Tips for listening are provided in the **Listening Highlight** section. Use the tips to better understand the video content.

AMERICAN VIBES
People, Places and Perspectives

Table of Contents

Everytown, USA

Texas—A Country All Its Own?

The West—Nature and the Native American Spirit

The Entertainment Capital of the World

Explore the "Emerald City"

American Voices
—Interviews

Map of the United States

Seattle

Seattle · Washington

Portland · Oregon

Boise · Idaho

Montana

Wyoming

North Dakota

Bismarck

South Dakota

Nebraska

Nevada

Utah

San Francisco · California

Las Vegas

Los Angeles

Williams · Arizona

Grand Canyon

Denver · Colorado

Kansas

Santa Fe · New Mexico

Oklahoma

Oklahoma City

Saint Jo

Texas

Austin

Grand Canyon

Williams

Santa Fe

Oswego

Port Clyde

Maine

Bar Harbor

Port Clyde

Vermont

New Hampshire

Boston

Massachusetts

Oswego

Rhode Island

New York

Connecticut

Minnesota

Wisconsin

Minneapolis

Michigan

New York City

Detroit

New Jersey

Chicago

Pennsylvania

Iowa

Indiana

Ohio

Maryland

Delaware

Illinois

Washington, D.C.

West Virginia

Virginia

New York City

Kansas City

Kentucky

Saint Louis

Missouri

North Carolina

Nashville

Tennessee

Arkansas

South Carolina

Memphis

Charleston

Georgia

Savannah

Alabama

Mississippi

Savannah

Louisiana

New Orleans

Florida

Miami

Austin

9

Chapter 1
Boston, Massachusetts

アメリカ北東部マサチューセッツ州最大の都市ボストン。ボストン大学の学生が愛用していた横長のカバンに由来するとされる「ボストンバッグ」や、メジャーリーグチームの名門ボストン・レッドソックスなど、ボストンは日本でもなじみ深い地名の一つでしょう。イギリスとの関係も深く、ボストンの南東にある町「プリマス」は、イギリスからの入植者が故郷の町にちなんで名付けました。ボストンはアメリカ独立戦争勃発のきっかけとなった「ボストン茶会事件」でも知られ、アメリカ発祥の地と言われています。

Warm-up

Work in pairs and answer the questions.

1. Locate Boston on the map on page 8.
2. Have you heard of Boston? What are your images of Boston?
3. What do you think the weather in Boston is like?

Vocabulary Preview

Match each word or phrase with the Japanese.

1. attract [　]

2. vibrant [　]

3. colonist [　]

4. rifle fire [　]

5. wound [　]

6. impose [　]

7. certificate [　]

8. dump [　]

a. 銃火	**b.** 入植者	**c.** 捨てる	**d.** 課す
e. 活気のある	**f.** 傷つける	**g.** 惹きつける	**h.** 証明書

Part 1 Getting to Know the Place

online video

Watch the video and answer the following questions about Boston.

① Which of the following was NOT an American first in Boston?

a. A subway system

b. A public library

c. A professional baseball team

② Which is true about Beacon Hill?

a. Some of the brownstones were built in the 1600s.

b. It is an affordable place to live.

c. It is a modern neighborhood with many young people.

③ What does Sandra say attracts many people to Boston?

a. The large number of young people

b. The large number of universities

c. The large number of jobs

4 What does Rich say is odd about Bostonians?

   a. Their way of interacting

   b. Their way of dressing

   c. Their way of talking

Part 2 ## Learning More

(online / video)

Watch the video about two historical events that are important in American history and complete the following notes.

The Boston Massacre

  ● *When?*   March 5th, [1]_____

  ● *Who were on the streets?*   [2]_____ soldiers

  ● *What did the colonists do?*   Threw some [3]_____, shouted some [4]_____ abuse

  ● *How did the British react?*   Returned with rifle [5]_____

                  ➡ Killed [6]_____ and wounded [7]_____

The Boston Tea Party = a [8]_____ protest that happened on Griffin's Wharf on [9]_____ 16th, 1773.

▶ Background

  ● The colonists were angry with the British for imposing [10]_____ without [11]_____. (The British were in [12]_____ in the 1760s and needed [13]_____.)

▶ The Stamp Act

  ● It imposed taxes on almost every kind of [14]_____.

▶ The colonists' protest

  ● So they dumped [15]_____ chests of fine British tea into the [16]_____.

Reading

DL 02   CD 02

Read the passage and answer the following questions.

The Solitary Founder of Boston

Aerial view of Boston Common

The Massachusetts tribe of Native Americans have lived around Shawmut, now Boston, since around 2400 BC. Then, in the early 17 century, English
5 Puritans came to the New World and built colonies. But, did you know there was an Englishman who settled there before the Puritans? Who was this first European settler in America? His
10 name was Reverend William Blaxton, and we have a pretty good idea of his personality, as well as the way he lived.

Blaxton was university educated and a priest in the Church of England. Along with a small colony of people, he left for the New World in 1623. After only a few years, the remainder of the colony returned to England. Blaxton was different.
15 He settled alone in an area that is now part of Boston Common. He chose the area because it had a spring that provided a lot of drinking water. This enabled him to plant the first apple orchards in North America. Blaxton was also known for having a large library of nearly 200 books.

In 1630, Reverend Blaxton heard that a colony on the other side of the river,
20 led by Governor Winthrop, was doing very badly. People were dying due to a lack of drinking water. Blaxton invited Winthrop, along with hundreds of settlers, to Shawmut. This was the end of his solitary life there. Only three years later, the population reached nearly 4,000. By late 1634, Blaxton decided to sell the land he legally owned and move on. Although Blaxton left when the city was young, there
25 is no doubt that his contribution helped establish the city of Boston. In a sense, we could call him "the real founder of Boston."

> **Notes**　Puritan「清教徒」　a small colony of people「少数の移民団」　the New World「新世界（大航海時代以降に
> ヨーロッパ人が発見した南北アメリカ大陸およびオーストラリア大陸をいう。特にアメリカ大陸を指すこと
> が多い）」　Boston Common「ボストン・コモン（ボストン中心部にあるアメリカ最古の公園）」　Governor
> Winthrop「ウィンスロップ知事（ピューリタンを新世界に導いた重要人物で、マサチューセッツ湾植民地の
> 初代知事）」

A **Answer if the following statements are true (T) or false (F).**

1. Boston was the name of the area before Shawmut.　　　　　[T / F]

2. Blaxton planted the first apple orchards in North America.　　[T / F]

3. Blaxton invited Winthrop and his colony to Shawmut.　　　　[T / F]

B **Answer the following questions.**

1. Why did Blaxton choose the area near the current Boston Common?

_____

2. Why do you think Blaxton decided to move away from Boston?

_____

入植の歴史からみるボストンとイギリス

　　赤煉瓦の美しい街並みが印象的なボストンは、札幌と同じくらいの緯度にあり、日本と同様に四季を楽しむことができます。ボストンは「アメリカ初」と言われる様々な公共施設を有する都市でもあり、まさにアメリカ発祥の地と言えます。

　アメリカ合衆国北東部の6州（メイン州、ニューハンプシャー州、バーモント州、マサチューセッツ州、ロードアイランド州、コネティカット州）をニューイングランド地方と呼びますが、ボストンを中心都市とするこの地方は、ピルグリム・ファーザーズと呼ばれるイギリス系の入植者によって開拓されました。1620年、彼らはメイフラワー号に乗ってイギリスを出発しアメリカに到着しますが、そこで彼らを待っていたのは厳寒の冬でした。もともとその地域に居住していたアメリカ先住民のワンパノアグ族は、ピルグリム・ファーザーズに食料を提供して支援したと言われています。これに感謝したピルグリム・ファーザーズは翌1621年、アメリカでの初の収穫を記念して、先住民達を招いて3日間の祝宴を開きました。これが現在の感謝祭（Thanksgiving）の起源と言われています。こうしてピルグリム・ファーザーズはワンパノアグ族と平和条約を結びますが、近隣に住むマサチューセッツ族をはじめとする他の部族とは敵対します。その後、ワンパノアグ族との平和条約を破って彼らの土地を奪います。激しい抗争とヨーロッパからもたらされた疫病のため、多くの先住民が命を落としました。

　このようにイギリス系植民者とボストンには密接な関係があり、それが言語にも反映されています。ボストン出身（ボストニアン）のケネディ大統領や俳優のマット・ディモンなどはイギリス英語に近いボストン訛りの英語を話します。特徴として、母音の後のrを発音しないnon-rhotic accentなどが挙げられます。（例: floor → fl'ɔɚ［米国英語］/ fl'ɔː［英国英語］）

The Mayflower, which carried pilgrims from England

American Voices #1

What are students in Boston like?
Meet the soccer team of Bunker Hill
Community College.

online / video
online / audio

DL 03   CD 03

A **Who said it? Match the person with what was said.**

 **1** [   ]    **2** [   ]    **3** [   ]

a. I met different people from around the world.

b. You could dream bigger.

c. Everybody played soccer. It was like a religion.

B **Watch the video again. Which of the following did Scott say?**

a. I think winning is the most important when you play sports.

b. I helped a lot of students because I am an immigrant myself.

c. American soccer is definitely on its way up.

C **Share your ideas with your classmates.**

1. What do you think you would miss most if you lived abroad?

2. Scott says, "if you want the players to perform well, they need to enjoy what they are doing." Do you agree? In sports, should the main goal be to have fun? Why or why not?

Listening Highlight

英語学習では、英語圏出身のネイティブによる音声をモデルにしていることが多いのではないでしょうか。しかしアメリカで耳にする英語は、サッカーの選手達が話す英語のように実に多様です。たとえば在米7年になるエルサルバドル出身の選手は、スペイン語なまりの英語を話しています。スペイン語の母音は"aeiou"の5個で、日本語の5個の母音「あいうえお」とほぼ同じと言われています。また、スペイン語ではsが濁らないため、"7 years"や"visit"の[z]の発音が[s]に聞こえますね。

16

Chapter 2

Maine

メイン州は、アメリカ北東部ニューイングランド地方に位置し、紀元前から先住民が居住していました。この地を初めて訪れたヨーロッパ人は、11世紀頃にやってきたアイスランドのバイキングだと言われています。その後1604年にフランス人が、1607年にはイギリス人が到着し、1620年代にイギリス人が沿岸に定住するようになりました。雄大な自然に恵まれたメイン州の州旗には、州の動物（state animal）であるヘラジカが描かれています。また、漁業や農業が盛んで、ロブスターの水揚げ量はアメリカ最大、野生のブルーベリーは世界一の収穫量を誇っています。

Warm-up

Work in pairs and answer the questions.

1. Locate Bar Harbor on the map on page 8.
2. Would you like to live in the city or a place with a lot of nature?
3. Do you like seafood? Give examples of what you like most.

Vocabulary Preview

Match each word or phrase with the Japanese.

1. moose   [   ]   5. bait   [   ]
2. explode   [   ]   6. distinguished   [   ]
3. teeming with   [   ]   7. depleted   [   ]
4. generate   [   ]   8. high-paying   [   ]

a. (釣りの) 餌	**b.** ヘラジカ	**c.** 枯渇した	**d.** 激増する
e. 給料のよい	**f.** 生み出す	**g.** 際立った	**h.** 〜でいっぱいの

Part **1**   ## Getting to Know the Place   online video

Watch the video and answer the following questions about Maine.

1 Which of the following is NOT true about Maine?

   a. Most people live outside the cities.
   b. It is famous for lobster.
   c. The people are in touch with nature.

2 What does Chrissy NOT say about the people in the back-to-the-land movement?

   a. They have corporate jobs.
   b. They grow their own food.
   c. They are looking to simplify their lives.

3 Which is true about Bar Harbor?

   a. It is very busy in summer.
   b. It is very busy in winter.
   c. Christmas is the biggest celebration.

④ Which is NOT true about Stephen King?

   a. He is a writer of horror.

   b. His stories have yet to be made into a movie.

   c. He has written more than 50 novels.

Part 2 ▸ **Learning More**

   (online / video)

Watch the video about the lobster business in Maine, and then complete the following notes.

How the lobster business works

Lobstermen get paid as little as 2-3 dollars a ¹_____, but the price escalates up to ²_____ dollars at a restaurant.

➡ *The reason*:
For every dollar a lobsterman gets, ³_____ to ⁴_____ dollars more are generated for related businesses (dealers, processors, restaurants, stores and ⁵_____ and tackle shops)

Co-founder of Luke's Lobster, Ben Conniff

● *Mission*   To bring the ⁶_____ ⁷_____ seafood to cities around the world

● *Locations*   ⁸_____ locations in the US, and ⁹_____ in Japan and 2 in Taiwan
     ➡ *Japanese market*: The country with the most ¹⁰_____ seafood taste, so it is ¹¹_____ to succeed there.

● *Sustainability*   For so long we ¹²_____ our natural resources, so sustainability is important.

A lobsterman, Mike

● *When he grew up….*
He used to hear ¹³_____ go by, and he wished he was on those boats rather than being in a ¹⁴_____.

● *His advice on life*
"Be your own ¹⁵_____."

Read the passage and answer the following questions.

Maine: Land of the Modern Homestead

Farmer in Maine

One quarter of all Americans have recently taken a pay cut or passed up a promotion to simplify their lives. This usually means they can spend more time
5 with family and friends. Some have decided, however, to leave the city and head to Maine. Land prices here are still reasonable, and if one works hard, one can make a living farming. In Maine, farmers under 35 have increased 40% in
10 recent years as compared to 1.5% for the nation as a whole. A primary concern of these young farmers is the environment. They want to raise sustainable crops and food that is free from chemicals.

These modern homesteaders, as they are often called, believe that happiness lies not in income, but in simplicity and community. The back-to-the-land movement
15 started with Scott Nearing, and his wife Helen, in the 1930s. Nearing saw the endless pursuit of money as empty. It seemed the more people acquired, the more they wanted. He came to Maine in the 1950s and paved the way for the next generation.

People during the cultural revolution of the late 60s and 70s took to his ideas naturally. Those young people did not want the suburban life of their parents, so
20 many took up communal farming. It was idealistic, but hard work. Many were surprised how much time it took simply to heat the house or prepare dinner. By the time the boom economy of the 1980s arrived, more than a few farmers left for corporate jobs and the life they had tried to avoid. It seemed their idealism was tied to economic realities.

25 No one knows how long the current movement will last. While urban life often satisfies needs for safety and security, time has shown that the values of community, simplicity, and sustainability are a powerful draw for the often exhausted city dweller.

Notes homestead「自作農場」　Scott Nearing「スコット・ニアリング（1883-1983; アメリカの経済学者、作家、政治活動家。妻のヘレンと共にシンプルな生活を実践。著作には *Living the Good Life*（1954）など）」 endless pursuit「際限ない追求」　boom economy「好景気」

A Answer if the following statements are true (T) or false (F).

1. Land in Maine is very expensive. [T / F]

2. Scott Nearing's goal was to make as much money as possible. [T / F]

3. Some farmers left in the 80s to take corporate jobs. [T / F]

B Answer the following questions.

1. What is a primary concern of young farmers in Maine?

   _____

2. What are two things homesteaders believe make people happy?

   _____

豊かな自然に抱かれて —メイン州とロブスター

　メイン州は、北海道と同じぐらいの緯度に位置しており、どこまでも続く海岸線と内陸部に広がる深い森に象徴される豊かな自然と、四季の変化がとても美しい街です。海辺の町ポート・クライドには19世紀に作られた灯台があり、トム・ハンクス主演の映画『フォレスト・ガンプ』(1994)にも登場します。メイン州は、フランス、イギリス、先住民が100年以上にわたって戦いを繰り広げた場所であり、アメリカ軍とイギリス軍が衝突した独立戦争の戦場でもありました。現在のメイン州は、全米で最も白人の多い地域の1つとしても知られ、約95％を白人が占めていると言われています。

Wild blueberries and a lobster roll

　メイン州といえばロブスターが有名です。世界各地からロブスター料理を求めて観光客が多数訪れていますが、パンにマヨネーズ和えのロブスターがたっぷりはさまったロブスターロールが特に人気です。獲れたてのロブスターを丸ごと1尾食べてみるのもよいでしょう。身が詰まって食べ応えのあるハードシェル・ロブスターは1年中提供されますが、ジューシーで柔らかい身が特徴のニューシェル・ロブスターがお目当てなら、収穫時期にあたる6月から11月頃に訪れるのがオススメです。

　ロブスター漁は1600年代から行われていると言われていますが、ロブスター産業を守るため、様々な法令と規制が実施されています。機械ではなく漁網罠で捕獲し、規格外のロブスターや、卵を持つメスは海に戻すなど、地域の海洋資源を次世代につなげていくための努力が行われています。しかし近年、地球温暖化による海水温の上昇のためにニューイングランド地方南部やニューヨーク州など一部の地域ではロブスターの水揚げ量が激減している地域もあり、より北部に位置するメイン州やカナダにおいても将来的な影響を懸念する声が挙がっています。

American Voices #2

Can you describe yourself in one word?
Before you watch the video, share your ideas
with your partner.

online / video
online / audio
DL 05   CD 05

A **Who said it? Match the person with what was said.**

 **1** [   ]

 **2** [   ]

 **3** [   ]

a. Complex. I guess the older I am, the more I realize I don't know.

b. Perfectionist. With everything I do, I'm never satisfied.

c. I'm really weird. I'm a really strange person.

B **Watch the video again. Which of the following did Isaac say?**

a. I love to smile when I'm happy. And I love to smile when I'm sad.

b. I love to smile when I'm happy but not when I'm sad.

c. I love to smile when I'm happy. And I love to cry when I'm sad.

C **Share your ideas with your classmates.**

1. Which of the 8 people do you think is most interesting? Tell why.

2. Evlondo says, "I have this unsatisfiable desire to just learn and learn." Do you have the same desire? What do you want to learn more about?

Listening Highlight

自分のことを一言で説明する表現はいろいろあります。Yobiは、良い意味で魅力的な「変わり者」を意味するquirkyという言葉を使って表現しています。そして "make the best out of any situation"「どんな状況でも最善を尽くす」が彼女のアピールポイントです。自分はcuriousであるというEvlondoは、休日も読書ばかりしている自分に恋人もうんざり…というエピソードを明かしています。アメリカでは、人と違うことや自分にしかできないことをアピールすることが、好意的に受け止められる土台があります。

Chapter 3
New York City 1

世界の政治や経済、ファッションや食文化の発信地ニューヨークは、アメリカ北東部ニューヨーク州最大の都市です。「メルティング・ポット」や「サラダ・ボウル」と呼ばれるこの街では、白人の割合は半数程度で、黒人・アフリカ系アメリカ人、ヒスパニック系やアジア系の人口も多いことで知られ、アメリカ先住民やアラスカ先住民といった少数民族も暮らしています。60以上の国や民族の人々によって、40以上の言語の新聞や雑誌が発行されており、その半分は英語以外の言語で、そして1割以上は2つ以上の言語で書かれていると言われています。

Warm-up

Work in pairs and answer the questions.

1. Locate New York City on the map on page 8.
2. What images do you have of New York City?
3. Would you like to visit New York City? Why or why not?

Vocabulary Preview

Match each word or phrase with the Japanese.

1. adapt to   [   ]   5. eclectic   [   ]
2. majestic   [   ]   6. counterculture   [   ]
3. time and again   [   ]   7. house band   [   ]
4. cobblestone   [   ]   8. define   [   ]

a. 何度も	**b.** 定義づける	**c.** お抱えバンド	**d.** 対抗文化、若者文化
e. 荘厳な	**f.** 多岐にわたる	**g.** ～になじむ	**h.** （道路舗装用の）丸石

Part 1 — Getting to Know the Place online / video

Watch the video and answer the following questions about New York City.

1 How many people pass through Times Square each year?

   a. 360,000

   b. 470,000

   c. 131,000,000

2 What does Alex say might be scary at first?

   a. The people

   b. The pace

   c. The prices

3 Which is true about the Empire State Building?

   a. It was built in 11 years.

   b. It is 102 stories.

   c. It was the tallest building for 90 years.

4 What does Alexandra NOT give as a reason for liking the East Village?

  a. The artists

  b. The eclectic crowd

  c. It is posh.

Part 2 Learning More

(online / video)

Watch the video about the area called Greenwich Village, and then complete the following notes.

> *Greenwich Village* = the center of 1960s ¹_____

Music

- *Café Wha?*   Bob Dylan ²_____ on the door in ³_____.
  The ⁴_____ band was Jimi Hendrix.
- There is a building where Bob Dylan once lived. ➡ He moved to ⁵_____.

▶ *NYC's musical history*

- ⁶_____ and jazz were created in the early ⁷_____ century.
- Also famous for rock, hip-hop, ⁸_____, funk and pop
  ➡ Famous musicians: Lady ⁹_____, the Ramones

Tree-lined Streets

- You don't worry about ¹⁰_____.
- There is a ¹¹_____ kind of feel.
- It's great to meet new people in the Village and play ¹²_____.
- A local resident, Jeffrey says…

  Low buildings make everybody ¹³_____.

Washington Square Park

- A lot of movies are ¹⁴_____.
- The center of New York University
- One of the best places for ¹⁵_____ to play in the summer

DL 06   CD 06

Read the passage and answer the following questions.

NYC: Pride

New York City has the largest LGBTQ population of any city in the United States. It is also widely recognized as the birthplace of the gay rights movement
5 because of what happened on June 28th, 1969 at the Stonewall Inn in Greenwich Village. The Stonewall Inn was typical for a gay bar at the time as it was owned by the Mafia, who paid bribes to the police
10 in exchange for ignoring that it was

The Stonewall Inn

selling alcohol without a license and allowing people to dance. It was a dirty place but options for gay patrons were limited in NYC at the time so they still came.

The Stonewall Inn ran smoothly as long as the Mafia paid bribes to the police, but at 1:20 that morning the police came to raid the bar. That night, the patrons
15 at the Stonewall Inn fought back. Quickly things escalated outside to where other New Yorkers fought against the police. This was a time when protests were everywhere. People fought for civil rights, women's rights and stopping the war in Vietnam. In the riot, the police were outnumbered by over 500 people. In the end, only 13 people ended up being arrested as the police just wanted to get out.
20 There was a second night of rioting and there was great support by other New Yorkers holding signs such as "Gay Power" and "Legalize Gay Bars."

Soon after, the first organization to use the word gay in their name, the Gay Liberation Front, started, and within six months NYC had its first gay newspaper, *GAY*. One year later, on the anniversary of the riots, the first Gay Pride marches
25 happened in NYC, LA, and Chicago. The struggle for social equality is not over for the LGBTQ community, but there are signs of progress every year. In 2019, Pride festivities supporters numbered 5 million, and the NYC Police Chief even offered an apology for the actions of the officers on that fateful night in 1969.

Notes   patron「常連客」   raid「急襲する」   outnumber「(〜よりも) 数でまさる」   Pride march「プライド・マーチ (LGBTQ文化を讃える毎年恒例のイベント。ニューヨークで行われるものはNYC Prideと呼ばれる)」

A Answer if the following statements are true (T) or false (F).

1. There were many gay bars in NYC before 1969.　　　　　[T / F]

2. Only gay people rioted in the Stonewall riots.　　　　　[T / F]

3. In 2019, the NYC Police Chief apologized for the riots in 1969.　[T / F]

B Answer the following questions.

1. Who owned typical gay bars in NYC in the 1960s?

_____

2. Give three examples of protests that were common at the time, other than the gay rights movement.

_____

American Eyes

脈々と続く移民の歴史

　　現在のニューヨーク市にあたる地域には、先史時代から先住民が居住しており、17世紀以降、オランダ人を中心とするヨーロッパ人の入植が始まるまで、狩猟や農業をしながら豊かな暮らしをしていました。先住民の土地の入手を目的とする入植者達は、物々交換を経て、土地の購入を実現させようとします。しかし、そもそも物や土地を「所有する」という概念のない先住民との平等な交渉ができるわけはなく、双方の軋轢が生じ、オランダ人やイギリス人などのヨーロッパ系白人による弾圧、戦争を経て、多くの部族が絶滅しました。ニューヨークには、ワシントンD.C.にある国立アメリカ・インディアン博物館の分館（ジョージ・グスタフ・ヘイ・センター）があり、先住民との歴史を学ぶことができます。

　　このように、ニューヨークもアメリカの他の地域と同様に、先住民の犠牲と移民の歴史の上に成り立っている街なのです。ニューヨーク湾内のエリス島には移民のための入国管理事務所があり、ニューヨークは、1892年から1924年までのおよそ30年間で推定1,700万人の移民を迎えたアメリカの玄関口でもありました。

Ellis Island Immigration Museum

　　ニューヨーカー達は、多様な背景を持つ人々の集まりです。ニューヨークの街のよい点を尋ねると、様々な文化や人はもちろん、多様性を積極的に受け入れる懐の深さや、多種多様な食べ物が魅力であるという話を耳にするのではないでしょうか。一方悪い点は、物価が高い、日々の生活がカオスである、地下鉄が予定通りに運行しないことがあるといったことが挙げられるようです。多様な文化を持つ人々との出会いは、様々な価値観との出会いでもあります。アメリカ文化への同化が求められた「メルティング・ポット」の時代から、多様な価値観が共存する「サラダ・ボウル」に変化している昨今は、予測できないカオスを楽しむ遊び心も、ニューヨーカー達の必需品なのかもしれません。

American Voices #3

What is happiness?
Before you watch the video,
share your ideas with your partner.

online / video
online / audio

 DL 07   CD 07

A Who said it? Match the person with what was said.

 **1** [   ]    **2** [   ]    **3** [   ]

a. Happiness is the absence of fear.

b. Happiness for me is stillness.

c. My dog Sam here is a good friend of mine.

B Watch the video again. Which of the following did Chrissy NOT say?

a. Happiness is being accepted in the community and living alone.

b. Happiness is having a family in a place where our lives are not so busy.

c. Happiness is having fulfilling work or being able to learn things that make life feel interesting.

C Share your ideas with your classmates.

1. What are you doing when you are most happy? Playing sports? Traveling? Reading?

2. Yobi says, "You can't make anyone else happy unless you are happy." Do you agree or can you make people happy even if you are not?

Listening Highlight

幸せの定義にはいろいろありますが、Jay Mohrの "when I'm not chasing anything, it's when I'm really happy" という表現は興味深く、彼の独特の人生観を感じさせるものとなっています。現状に満足する、内側から幸福感を感じる―という考え方は、Yobiの "it all comes from within." や、Sandraの "Inner peace." という発言とも通じるものがあります。Sandraは友人に食事を作って美味しいと喜んでもらえたときに幸せを感じるとも語っており、日常の何気ない瞬間に幸せを見つける彼女の生き方が伝わってきます。

Chapter 4
New York City 2

1625年、ニューヨーク市にあたる地域を最初に植民地としたのはオランダで、当時の地名はニューアムステルダムでした。その後、オランダがイギリスとの戦いに破れたことで、ニューアムステルダムはイギリス領となりました。ニューアムステルダムは、イギリスのヨーク公（後のジェームズ2世）の名を取って、ニューヨークと改名されたのです。マンハッタン島の南に位置するブルックリン（Brooklyn）もオランダ由来の地名で、ニューヨーク市の中でも最も歴史がある地区です。

Warm-up

Work in pairs and answer the questions.

1. What is your favorite park and why?
2. Do you know who John Lennon is? Can you name any of his songs?
3. Can you name any movies that were filmed in New York City?

Match each word or phrase with the Japanese.

1. equated with   [   ]
2. admire   [   ]
3. tribute to   [   ]
4. rush   [   ]

5. aggressive   [   ]
6. foodie   [   ]
7. literally   [   ]
8. co-exist   [   ]

| a. 称賛する | b. 食通 | c. 攻撃的な | d. 共存する |
| e. 急ぐ | f. 文字通り | g. ～への賛辞 | h. ～と同一視される |

Part 1 Getting to Know the Place online video

Watch the video and answer the following questions about New York City.

① How many people walk over the Brooklyn Bridge every day?

a. 2,600

b. 4,000

c. 120,000

② What sport does Isaac like to play in Central Park?

a. Soccer

b. Softball

c. Frisbee

③ The Bow Bridge is often in...

a. historical movies.

b. crime dramas.

c. romantic movies.

(4) Only 14% of visitors to Central Park are...

   a. from other countries.

   b. visiting for the first time.

   c. exercising or training.

 Part 2 Learning More   (online video)

Watch the video about what the local people say about New York City, and then complete the following notes.

The vibe of the city

- *What makes NY great*:   the energy, the people and the ^{1}_____

   ➡ He never knew walking was a ^{2}_____ sport.

- New Yorkers are ^{3}_____.
- They are just always ^{4}_____.

   ➡ They sometimes come off as ^{5}_____, but they have to keep moving to ^{6}_____ in what they're doing.

Food

- Her favorite is ^{7}_____ pizza.

   ➡ Tastes ^{8}_____ and no charge for ^{9}_____ cheese

- He likes to try the ^{10}_____ new restaurant or different types of ^{11}_____.

   ➡ Goes Chinatown, Korea town and ^{12}_____ ^{13}_____

Alexandra's advice for people coming to NY

- "Save a lot of ^{14}_____."

  "Cook at home and go ^{15}_____ shopping."

- It's still a community where people with contrasting beliefs co-exist.

   ➡ "Have your heart and mind ^{16}_____ to new experiences and new ^{17}_____."

Read the passage and answer the following questions.

Pride through Diversity in New York City

New York City is impossible to describe. You have to go there. You have to live it. People talk about the energy, but how is it different from any other big city? It might
5 help to start with some statistics that show you who you might meet or pass by on the street on any given day.

People in Chinatown, New York

Let's start with the basics. New York City is made up of five boroughs: Manhattan, Brooklyn, Queens, The Bronx, and
10 Staten Island. Manhattan, although the smallest by far, is the place you are most likely to see in the movies and is where the most money is made. New York has been the home of the most billionaires in the world for the past five years and most live on that little island.

Money may be what fuels the economy, but it's the people who energize the
15 streets. New York has been the largest city in the United States every year since 1790. The city is by far the leading place for immigrants to settle. There are more than 3 million foreign born residents of NYC and over 800 different languages are spoken, making it the most linguistically diverse city on the planet.

So, who are the New Yorkers? Racially, they can be seen as one of four main
20 groups. White Americans are the majority with 42% followed by Black Americans at 24%, and then Hispanic and Asian Americans at almost 15% each. This stands in stark contrast to the rest of America where those numbers reach 60% white, 18% Hispanic, 12% Black or African-American and only 6% Asian-American.

When New Yorkers are asked overseas where they are from, the answer is
25 often New York. They do not say the United States because New York looks and feels so much different from the rest of the country. New Yorkers are proud that, in this walking city, you can meet people from any country in the world on any given day.

Notes fuel「刺激する」 by far「群を抜いて」 linguistically diverse「言語的に多様である」
in stark contrast to「～と対極的に」 walking city「歩行者の多い街」

A Answer if the following statements are true (T) or false (F).

1. Manhattan is the largest borough.   [T / F]

2. There are 3 million languages spoken in New York City.   [T / F]

3. In NYC, white Americans are the majority with 60%.   [T / F]

B Answer the following questions.

1. Describe what kind of place Manhattan is.

_____

2. Give a reason for why New Yorkers feel NYC is different from the rest of the USA.

_____

自由の女神が見つめているもの

　世界遺産にも登録されている自由の女神は、マンハッタンの南に位置するバッテリー・パークから、フェリーに乗って15分ほどのリバティー島にあります。徐々に右手に見えてくる自由の女神像は圧巻で、アメリカに来たことを実感します。Statue of Libertyの名前で知られる自由の女神の正式名称は、Liberty Enlightening the World（世界を照らす自由）で、実は「女神」という表現はありません。アメリカ合衆国の独立100周年を記念して、1884年にフランスからアメリカに贈られました。大きな像は解体して船で運ばれ、アメリカで2年がかりで完成させました。それを伝えた日本の郵便報知新聞（のちの報知新聞）が、像を「女神」と訳したと言われています。

　自由の女神は、アメリカの自由や民主主義、そして移民の国の象徴とされています。その女神像の台座には、ユダヤ系アメリカ人の詩人エマ・ラザラス（Emma Lazarus, 1849-1887）の一節が次のように刻まれています。

Give me your tired, your poor,
Your huddled masses yearning to breathe free,
The wretched refuse of your teeming shore.
Send these, the homeless, tempest-tost to me,
I lift my lamp beside the golden door!

Statue of Liberty seen from ferry

「疲れし者、貧しき者を我に与えよ。自由の空気を吸わんと熱望する人たちよ——。身を寄せ合う哀れな人たちよ。住む家なく、嵐にもまれし者を我に送りたまえ。我は、黄金の扉にて灯を掲げん」
（*The New Colossus,* 1883より）

　移民大国アメリカでは、移民の受け入れや反移民政策などの問題がますます重要な争点になってきています。移民と一言で言っても、現在はこれまで以上に国籍や個々の状況が多様化しており、奴隷として連れてこられた人々の子孫や、保留地に追いやられ、絶滅の危機にある民族なども、雇用や生活の格差に直面し、不自由な生活を強いられています。エマ・ラザラスの詩の意味が、改めて問われているのではないでしょうか。

American Voices #4

What image do you think Americans have of Japan? Before you watch the video, share your ideas with your partner.

online video
online audio

🎧 DL 09   💿 CD 09

A Who said it? Match the person with what was said.

 **1** [   ]

 **2** [   ]

 **3** [   ]

a. I enjoy *Naruto, Bleach* and *Fullmetal Alchemist.*

b. Tokyo is a fashion capital.

c. Everything is kind of like "kawaii" cute.

B Watch the video again. Which of the following did Lauryn say?

a. Japan seems like a peaceful place with kind and orderly people.

b. Japan seems like a peaceful place that's in touch with their ancestry and their spirituality.

c. Japan seems like an exciting place that's abundant with beautiful nature and spiritual spots.

C Share your ideas with your classmates.

1. Did you hear what you expected? What surprised you? What was left out?

2. Sergio says, "I love samurai movies and I also love alternative cinema." How much do you know about Japanese movie history? Who are your favorite actors?

Listening Highlight

Samは、ルームメイトの日本人が、初対面のときや同居中も、そして引っ越すときにもくれたというgiftについて語っています。Samの "… we share the space. This is not my home, it's our home." という言葉から、日本とアメリカの贈り物文化の違いが読み取れます。日本では、初対面の挨拶などで「お世話になる」ことへ感謝のしるしに贈り物を持参することがよくあります。しかし異なる文化では、贈り物を渡す行為について疑問に思われることもあります。

"Our lives begin to end the day we become silent about things that matter."
- Martin Luther King, Jr

Chapter 5

Washington, D.C.

アメリカ合衆国の首都であるワシントンD.C.（コロンビア特別区）は、いずれの州にも属さない特別区です。国会議事堂やホワイトハウスがあり、国際的にも重要な役割を持つ世界銀行や国際通貨基金（IMF）の本部、そして連邦捜査局（FBI）などもあります。ワシントンD.C.の中心部にあるポトマック公園では、1912年に日本から桜が贈られたことを記念して、毎年春に全米桜祭りが行われ、満開の桜の下でパレードや打ち上げ花火などの賑やかなイベントが催されます。

Warm-up

Work in pairs and answer the questions.

1. Locate Washington, D.C. on the map on page 8.
2. Do you ever think about politics?
3. What issues are you most concerned about?

Vocabulary Preview

Match each word with the Japanese.

1. cynical [ ]
2. corruption [ ]
3. optimistic [ ]
4. poll [ ]

5. commemorate [ ]
6. Beltway [ ]
7. gentrification [ ]
8. advocate [ ]

a. 世論調査	**b.** 楽観的な	**c.** 汚職、腐敗	**d.** 支持する、主張する
e. 高級化	**f.** 皮肉な	**g.** 追悼する	**h.** （ワシントンDCを取りまく）環状道路

Part 1

Getting to Know the Place

online/video

Watch the video and answer the following questions about Washington, D.C.

1 What is NOT mentioned as people's opinions about D.C.?

a. It runs on greed and corruption.
b. It is where your voice can be heard.
c. It is a shopping capital.

2 Josh says that D.C. is a center of...

a. culture, history, and monumentalism.
b. art, music, and institutionalism.
c. shopping, cuisine, and commercialism.

3 Where did Martin Luther King's "I Have a Dream" speech take place?

a. The Jefferson Memorial
b. The Lincoln Memorial
c. The Vietnam Veterans Memorial

4 What has changed for Sam since moving to D.C.?

   a. She thinks about politics more.

   b. She thinks about politics less.

   c. She never thinks about politics.

Part 2   **Learning More**   (online / video)

Watch the video about what the three people describe Washington, D.C., and then complete the following notes.

How People Describe D.C.

- *Her original plan*:   Not going to live [1]_____ the Beltway
  - ➡ Beltway = being sort of [2]_____ from the rest of America
- *Years later…*   Still here and bought her [3]_____ [4]_____
- Very [5]_____ people are actually born and raised in D.C.
- She's from [6]_____ and misses having that identity.

- People come from all over the world.
  - ➡ The best people with the [7]_____ ideas
- D.C. is the center of [8]_____ in the US.
- If you stay here long, you will understand how the ideas work themselves into [9]_____.

- D.C. was the "[10]_____ City."
  - ➡ Now because of gentrification it's the [11]_____ City. No, it's the Cappuccino City, more milk than espresso.

- D.C. is called "Chocolate City" because it's a minority [12]_____ city.
  - ➡ [13]_____ Americans make up the majority of the population.

Read the passage and answer the following questions.

Washington, D.C.: Home to Political Speech

Protesting is a way of life in Washington, D.C. It makes sense as it is the seat of power in this country and if any laws or policies change, this will be where it happens. Some of the largest protests in the history of the United States have happened recently in D.C. The biggest ever was the 2017 Women's March, which was estimated to have between 3-4 million in attendance. March for Our Lives,

The Women's March held in January 2017

10 a protest over gun violence drew 1-2 million in 2018. In 1995, the Million Man March reached almost a million protestors in an effort to raise awareness of the lives of African American men in America.

Protestors see themselves as patriots who are trying to change things for the better. Many conservatives see protestors as troublemakers who are trying to 15 change things that do not need to be changed. Does protesting really change anything though? Isn't it better just to vote in elections? The Moratorium to End the War in Vietnam is something we should examine to answer this question. In November of 1969, around a half million people protested outside the White House. President Nixon, at the time, said there was no way he would be affected by the 20 demonstrations. Privately, however, he admitted on tape that he did watch them on TV and was moved. He even met secretly with protestors at 4:00 a.m. on a morning in 1970.

Whether or not Nixon directly changed his policy on Vietnam because of the protestors is not clear. Surely though, he was made aware that a great many 25 Americans disagreed with his policies. If you had been alive in 1969, would you have joined the march to stop the war or would you have stayed silent? While some see silence as golden, others see it as complicity. Is there any cause that makes you want your voice to be heard?

Notes seat of power「権力の座」　patriot「愛国者」　conservative「保守的な人、保守派」　President Nixon「ニクソン大統領（アメリカ合衆国第37代大統領 [1969-1974]。当時泥沼化していたベトナム戦争の幕引きを図ったが苦戦した)」　complicity「共犯、共謀」

A Answer if the following statements are true (T) or false (F).

1. Protests have become smaller in recent years.　　　　　　　[T / F]

2. The largest protest ever was the 2017 Women's March.　　　[T / F]

3. President Nixon did not watch TV.　　　　　　　　　　　　[T / F]

B Answer the following questions.

1. Why are there so many protests in Washington D.C.?

_____

2. Give two examples of how we know that Nixon paid attention to the protests.

_____

現代に引き継がれる"I Have a Dream"の思い

　　　首都ワシントンでは、1963年に人種差別の撤廃を求めて行われた大規模なデモ（ワシントン大行進）の最中に、キング牧師（1929-1968）がリンカー

Audiences listen to the President speaking at the Lincoln Memorial in 2013, commemorating the 50th anniversary of the "I Have a Dream" speech.

ン記念堂の前で演説 "I Have a Dream" を行いました。翌年には公民権法が成立し、法や制度面での差別の是正が大幅に進みましたが、それまでの道のりは平坦ではありませんでした。1862年のリンカーン大統領による奴隷解放宣言により奴隷制は廃止されたものの、実際の黒人の生活は「自由・平等」の理念からはかけ離れたものでした。100年近く経った1955年にある事件が起こります。アラバマ州在住の黒人女性のローザ・パークスが、バスで運転手から白人に席を譲る指示を受けますが、従わなかったために逮捕されました。これを受けて始まったバス乗車へのボイコット運動を指揮した中心人物が、キング牧師でした。彼は差別撤廃を目指す公民権運動を全米各地で指導し、先述のワシントン大行進には約20万人を超える人々が参加しました。

　　一方で、その後も多くの文学作品や映画で黒人問題の根深さが取り上げられています。アメリカ初の黒人ノーベル文学賞作家トニ・モリスン（1931-2019）は、『青い眼がほしい』（1970）の中で、白人社会の価値観の普遍化に疑問を呈しています。より最近では、NASAのマーキュリー計画（1958年から1963年にかけて実施されたアメリカで最初の有人宇宙飛行計画）を支えた黒人初の女性計算手の映画『ドリーム』（2016）で、差別と戦う黒人のサクセスストーリーが描かれました。作家や公民権運動家であったジェイムズ・ボールドウィン（1924-1987）の原作を映画化した『私はあなたのニグロではない』（2016）は、差別の歴史を振り返るだけでなく、そもそも差別がどのようにして作られるのかといった根本的な問題を提示したことで話題作となりました。近年黒人問題だけでなく移民問題やネイティブ・アメリカンの問題にも直面するアメリカにとって、無知や先入観が作り出す「差別」との戦いは永遠のテーマであると言えるでしょう。

American Voices #5

What is a friend?
Before you watch the video,
share your ideas with your partner.

online / video
online / audio
DL 11   CD 11

A Who said it? Match the person with what was said.

 **1** [   ]    **2** [   ]    **3** [   ]

a. A friend will pick me up from the airport even though I may be an hour late.

b. A friend would be somebody I would let babysit my kid.

c. A friend is someone who is there no matter what happens in your life.

B Watch the video again. Which of the following did Banna say?

a. A friend warns you of all your flaws and shortcomings, but is there for you.

b. A friend accepts all your flaws and shortcomings, but is there for you.

c. A friend never cares about all your flaws and shortcomings.

C Share your ideas with your classmates.

1. Sandra says, "blood does not connect you, the heart does." Are your best friends in your family or people you are not related to?

2. If you find your friend doing something that isn't good, what would you do?

Listening Highlight

皆さんは、自分の友達について説明するときに、どのような表現を使いますか。インタビューでは、"someone who is there no matter what happens"、"somebody who will be there when you need them"といった表現が使われており、見返りなしに助けを差し伸べ、寄り添ってくれる友達を大切に思う気持ちが感じ取れます。"A friend in need is a friend indeed."「まさかの時の友こそ真の友」という諺がありますが、アメリカも日本も、「友達」に対する考え方は共通なのかもしれません。

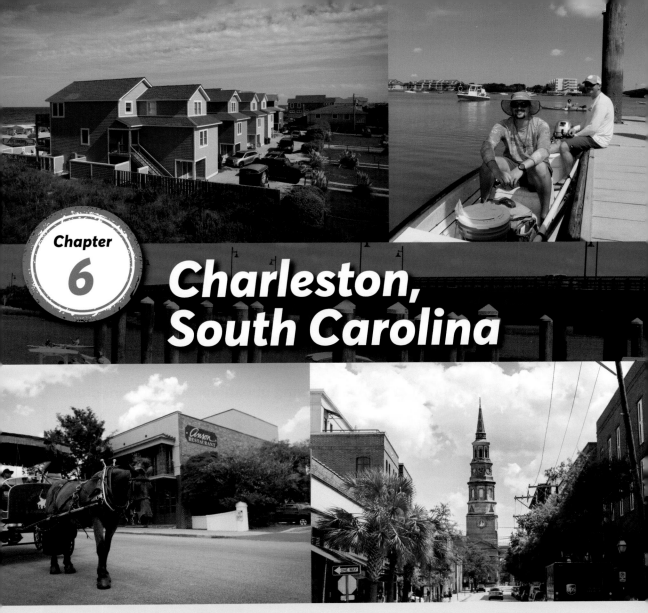

Chapter 6
Charleston, South Carolina

チャールストンは、アメリカ南東部サウスカロライナ州に位置し、南北戦争の発端となった場所として知られています。18世紀の奴隷貿易によって繁栄した港町で、石畳の路地や道路沿いのヤシの木、美しい歴史的建造物、多くの教会などを見て楽しむことができます。『トム・ソーヤーの冒険』(1878) の物語に出てくるような、外輪式蒸気船に乗って、チャールストンの沖合にあるサムター要塞にも行ってみましょう。アメリカ南部の負の歴史を現代に伝える場所として、今なお国内外から多くの人々が見学に訪れています。

Warm-up

Work in pairs and answer the questions.

1. Locate Charleston on the map on page 8.
2. Where would be your ideal place to live? Think about its weather, location and people.
3. What comes to your mind when you think of a historical town in Japan?

Match each word or phrase with the Japanese.

1. delightful   [   ]
2. denomination   [   ]
3. steeple   [   ]
4. plumbing   [   ]

5. slave trade   [   ]
6. hazardous   [   ]
7. fort   [   ]
8. petroleum   [   ]

a. 危険な	**b.** 配管	**c.** 宗派	**d.** 石油
e. 愉快な	**f.** 尖塔	**g.** 奴隷貿易	**h.** 砦

Part 1

Getting to Know the Place

online / video

Watch the video and answer the following questions about Charleston.

1 How does James describe winter in Charleston?

  a. Humid

  b. Mild

  c. Delightful

2 Charleston is also known as...

  a. the Slavery City.

  b. the Holy City.

  c. the Charm City.

3 What year did James say his house was built?

  a. 1890

  b. 1980

  c. 1770

4 What happened at Fort Sumter?

a. The Civil War started.

b. The Revolutionary War started.

c. The slave trade took place.

Part 2 Learning More

(online / video)

Watch the video about the Intracoastal Waterway, and then complete the following notes.

Intracoastal Waterway

- *Where?*
  Runs from [1]_____ all the way down to [2]_____

  ➡ Nearly [3]_____km down the [4]_____ Coast

- *How It began*
  Almost as [5]_____ as the US itself

  Sailing along the Atlantic was [6]_____.

  ➡ Needed to find a way to safely move [7]_____

- *Today*
  A large amount of the traffic is by [8]_____ boaters.

▶ *A day at the Intracoastal Waterway...*

- *What is Zach doing?*

  "We're [9]_____, trying to catch some [10]_____."

- *What kind of fish can be caught?*

  "We get a lot of sea [11]_____.

  Every now and then, you might get a rare fish called "tarpon.""

- *Does Zach eat these shrimp?*

  "We are [12]_____ going to eat them but we [13]_____.

  We're going to use them for [14]_____ today.""

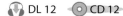

Read the passage and answer the following questions.

The Confederate Flag and Charleston

The flag of the Confederate States of America causes divisive reactions to people in the United States. To understand why, one needs to examine what it symbolizes.

Confederate flag and gravestone

5　The Civil War, from 1861-1865, was America's bloodiest war where between 620,000 to 750,000 lost their lives. That is more than all the other wars fought by the USA combined. There is debate whether the war was fought because of states' rights or to abolish slavery. It is important though to realize
10　that slavery was one of the primary rights the Southern states wanted to protect.

According to a Pew Research poll, more than half of Americans believe that the Civil War is relevant to American life and political thought today. A symbol of the war can be seen as positive or negative depending on who you ask. Black Americans view the Confederate flag negatively 41% of the time whereas white
15　Americans have this feeling only 29% of the time. This is not surprising as blacks were enslaved in the Confederate states. Those who graduate college view the flag negatively 46% of the time whereas those with only a high school education have this view only 18% of the time. Positive views of the flag are held by 14% of those with a high school education or less. This number drops to 5% when
20　surveying college graduates.

Confederate General Robert E. Lee is still one of the most respected historical figures from the war. He fought bravely for the Southern cause, but when the war ended, he swore to uphold the Constitution of the United States. He never flew the Confederate flag again, not even at the Southern college where he became president.
25　He even sent specific instructions that none of the attendees to his funeral should wear the Confederate uniform. Lee also made sure that he was not buried in uniform or with the flag. He wanted to make it clear that the Civil War was a thing of the past.

Notes　the Confederate States of America「アメリカ連合国（南北戦争直前の1861年に、アメリカ合衆国を脱退し南部諸州が結成。奴隷制の維持や自由貿易を主張したが、南北戦争終結と同時に消滅した）」　divisive「対立した」　Pew Research poll「ピュー研究所（アメリカの大手シンクタンク）の世論調査」　General Robert E. Lee「ロバート・エドワード・リー（1807-1870; アメリカ連合国の軍事令官として活躍）」　uphold「支持する」　the Southern college「南部の大学（ここではヴァージニア州にあるワシントン・アンド・リー大学を指す）」

Ⓐ Answer if the following statements are true (T) or false (F).

1. Slavery was the only reason the Civil War was fought. 　　　[T / F]

2. In the Civil War, many enslaved people fought to protect the rights of Southern states. 　　　[T / F]

3. General Robert E. Lee refused to be buried in his Confederate uniform.

　　　[T / F]

Ⓑ Answer the following questions.

1. Name two groups that view the Confederate flag negatively.

_____

2. When the Civil War ended, how did Robert E. Lee's attitude toward the Confederate States change?

_____

南部の魅力 ―負の歴史と向き合いながら

　　植民地の都市として長い歴史を持つチャールストン。先住民との戦いの歴史だけではなく、黒人奴隷制度を巡って争った南北戦争での敗北は、その後の街の発展の大きな足かせとなりました。アメリカ本土に直接連れて来られた奴隷の約40万人のうち、実に4割をチャールストンが受け入れたと言われ、今も人種差別の問題が根強く残っています。

　　チャールストンでは、このような負の歴史を様々な博物館で学ぶことができます。奴隷の競売場跡に作られた旧奴隷市場博物館では、劣悪な環境の船で運ばれた奴隷の様子や、奴隷の年齢や体格で分けられた価格表、そして綿花や米、たばこなどのプランテーションでの過酷な労働状況を示す資料が展示されています。チャールストンには、アメリカ最古の博物館（チャールストン博物館）もあり、戦争の歴史や自然史に加え、地域の人々の芸術作品や生活を理解することもできます。

　　サウスカロライナ州と言えば、サザン・チャームと呼ばれるアメリカ南部独特の魅力も有名です。人々のゆったりとした暮らしぶり、マナーの良さ、家族の強い絆、手作りの食事、そして人々の温かいおもてなしの心（サザン・ホスピタリティ）などが、南部のイメージとして知られています。街を歩けば、Hi!と声をかけられることもしばしば。機会があれば、名物の南部料理を提供してくれるレストランにも立ち寄ってみたいものです。フライドチキンやナマズ料理、オクラのフライ、コーンブレッド、葉物野菜の煮込みなどに代表される南部料理は、過酷な奴隷制時代を経てアフリカ系アメリカ人が作り上げた「ソウルフード」でもあります。こうした素朴な料理と店員さんの気さくな接客で、お腹も心も満たされることでしょう。

Old Slave Mart Museum

American Voices #6

Let's meet James Scott, a historian and author, who specializes in the war in the Pacific.

online / video
online / audio
🎧 DL 13 ⦿ CD 13

A **Watch James' interview and check 2 things that match what he says.**

☐ He wanted to make a living by writing, and became a journalist.

☐ He began to write books soon after graduating from school.

☐ He thinks numbers are of primary importance in history.

☐ His first book was published in 2009.

☐ *Target Tokyo* was written about why Japan attacked Pearl Harbor.

B **Which of the following did James mention about his idea of history?**

a. The best stories are the ones of extraordinary people placed in ordinary circumstances.

b. The best stories are the ones of ordinary circumstances that make people extraordinary.

c. The best stories are the ones of ordinary people placed in extraordinary circumstances.

C **Share your ideas with your classmates.**

1. How often do you read? What kind of things do you like reading most and why?

2. Are you interested in history? If you could travel to any time period, what period would you travel to?

Listening Highlight

Jamesが指摘する通り、歴史は客観的な事実ではなく、一人一人の人間が作り出す物語であると言えるでしょう。事実、historyの語源はギリシャ語のhistoriaで、an account of one's inquiries, history, record, narrativeを意味する語でした。また、彼の話す英語には南部訛りの特徴があります。たとえばwriterは、[rai]よりも[ra:]に近い発音で、wからtまで、母音が鼻にかかった感じで柔らかく聞こえませんか。また、warやperformedのrを含む音節は、口ごもったようなworeやfourに近い音です。

46

Chapter 7

Savannah, Georgia

アメリカ南東部ジョージア州の古都サバンナは、アメリカ屈指の美しい街として知られています。南北戦争（1861-1865）以前の建物が立ち並ぶ長い歴史を持つこの街は、奴隷制による綿花プランテーションで繁栄しました。映画のロケ地としても有名で、『フォレスト・ガンプ』（1994）の冒頭ではトム・ハンクス扮する主人公がベンチに座りバスを待つシーンが、クリント・イーストウッド監督のミステリー映画『真夜中のサバナ』（1997）では美しく妖しいサバンナの街並みが登場します。

Warm-up

Work in pairs and answer the questions.

1. Locate Savannah on the map on page 8.
2. What images do you have of the American South?
3. Do you believe in ghosts? Why or why not?

47

Match each word or phrase with the Japanese.

1. declare independence   [   ]
2. grid   [   ]
3. historic landmark   [   ]
4. haunted   [   ]

5. cemetery   [   ]
6. general   [   ]
7. spare   [   ]
8. cause   [   ]

a. 将軍	**b.** 格子	**c.** 史跡	**d.** 幽霊の出る
e. 大義	**f.** とっておく、救う	**g.** 独立を宣言する	**h.** 共同墓地

Part 1   Getting to Know the Place   online video

Watch the video and answer the following questions about Savannah.

1 Which of the following is NOT a feature of Savannah?

   a. It is the first planned city in America.

   b. It has perfectly straight streets in a grid.

   c. Most of their parks are square in shape.

2 Why does Todd ask, "Where are the bodies?"

   a. He is going to River Street and is looking for friends.

   b. Savannah expanded on top of Native American burial grounds.

   c. There were recent attacks by pirates.

3 What is NOT mentioned about River Street?

   a. Tourists often go there first.

   b. There is good live music.

   c. It has secret spots that only locals know.

4 What are 3 things that James says he likes about Savannah?

  a. Food, history, and the Spanish moss.
  b. People, food, the relaxing atmosphere.
  c. Culture, politics, and the people.

Part 2 Learning More

(online / video)

Watch the video about history of Savannah seen from two perspectives, and then complete the following notes.

Marvin's favorite story of Savannah

- *How Savannah was spared*

  General Sherman came down to the South, and he [1]_____ down every city from Atlanta to [2]_____. But Savannah was the [3]_____ city that was [4]_____.

- *Possible Reasons*

  (1) He fell in [5]_____ with Savannah, and he [6]_____ it to President Lincoln as a [7]_____ gift.

  (2) His [8]_____ was from Savannah, and she didn't want to see it burned [9]_____.

Monuments debate

- Meaning of the monuments

  Monuments = To [10]_____ the Confederate dead.

  ➡ They fought and died for the South in the [11]_____ War

- Recent debate

▶ *For the monuments*

  The soldiers should be remembered because they [12]_____ and died for a [13]_____ they believed in.

▶ *Against the monuments*

  The monuments remind people of the [14]_____ to which they never want to return.

DL 14 CD 14

Read the passage and answer the following questions.

The Ghosts of Savannah

Savannah is full of ghosts. Passing beneath the Spanish moss, one can feel the paranormal walking the beautiful city streets. Perhaps not everyone can feel it,
5 but one thing is for sure: there are hundreds of ghost stories that people from Savannah can choose to tell.

Colonial Park Cemetery

War is a part of Savannah's past and they have not come out on the winning side. One example is the Siege of Savannah
10 during the Revolutionary War in 1779. French and American troops were defeated by the British who held the city until 1782.

Disease has also played a larger role here than in most other cities. In 1820, Savannah lost 10% of its population to yellow fever. Nine other epidemics followed; notably one in 1876 where over 1,000 lives were lost. Likewise, fire ravaged the city
15 in 1792 and again in 1820 destroying over 700 buildings and taking many lives.

Slavery has also played a large part in Savannah from when it was founded until the end of the Civil War. As if slavery itself were not scary enough, there is the story of the French ship that was sent to Savannah in 1854 to pick up 71 escaped slaves. On its way out to sea, it sank in the harbor. Sailors today have
20 stories of hearing voices speaking French when sailing past.

On top of all this, is the fact that Savannah was originally built on a Native American burial ground. Some bodies were never moved and are, at times, discovered during construction projects. Keen observers also note that Savannah has a lot fewer cemeteries in the center of town than it once had. Were those
25 bodies moved or simply built over?

Many believe that a peaceful death and a proper burial will lead to a restful afterlife. With all of the unfortunate events, and the untimely deaths they caused, it is no wonder the dead of Savannah seem so restless.

Notes paranormal「超常的な、科学的に説明できない」 Siege of Savannah「サバンナ包囲戦（アメリカ独立戦争中にサバンナの支配を巡ってイギリス軍とアメリカ・フランス連合軍が戦った）」 epidemic「伝染病」 ravage「破壊する」 restless「落ち着かない、鎮まらない」

A Answer if the following statements are true (T) or false (F).

1. There are many ghost stories about Savannah.　　　　　[T / F]

2. There was a World War I battle fought in Savannah.　　　[T / F]

3. We do not know where all the buried bodies are in Savannah.　[T / F]

B Answer the following questions.

1. Give four examples of how people in Savannah died untimely deaths.

_____

2. Why are sailors said to hear French being spoken in the harbor?

_____

計画都市サバンナ
―その影にある先住民の涙と奴隷制度の歴史

　アメリカ南部の歴史は、先住民族との争いと奴隷制度を抜きにしては語れないでしょう。後にジョージア州となる地域には、チェロキー族やクリーク族などのネイティブ・アメリカンが居住していました。1830年代にジョージア州で起こったゴールドラッシュで白人がチェロキー族の土地に乱入し、戦争を経て敗北したチェロキー族は、現在のオクラホマ州に強制移住を余儀なくされました。この出来事は「涙の旅路」と呼ばれ、その道中は過酷なものでした。移動させられたネイティブ・アメリカンの数は10万人にのぼり、そのうち15,000人ほどが亡くなったと推定されています。彼らの中にはクリスチャンも多く、「アメイジング・グレイス」を歌って励まし合ったと言われています。

　サバンナでは、1733年イギリスのジェームス・オグルソープを中心とする入植者達の到着後、計画的な都市計画が進められました。オグルソープはジョージア植民地の発展に貢献した人物として名高く、市内には銅像も建てられています。現在も健在である碁盤の目状の街を歩き、計画的に配置されたスクエアと呼ばれる22の公園を訪れれば、サバンナ独自の整然とした街並みを堪能できるでしょう。歴史に興味のある人は、黒人奴隷の犠牲の上に成立した巨万の富を象徴する邸宅や、北部に黒人を逃したと言われる地下トンネルのある教会もぜひ訪れてみてください。南部の街は、アメリカ建国の歴史と現代にもつながる様々な課題の縮図とも言えるのです。

Memorial in Savannah for James Edward Oglethorpe

American Voices #7

online / video
online / audio
DL 15   CD 15

Do you believe in love at first sight?
Before you watch the video,
share your ideas with your partner.

A Who said it? Match the person with what was said.

 1 [   ]    2 [   ]    3 [   ]

a. This person has an energy that attracts me.

b. Wow. I think I love her. And we hit it off and we're married.

c. I fall in love every single day. I'm not kidding.

B Watch the video again. Which of the following did Sergio say?

a. You don't know. There's so much of a surprise.
It's not an acknowledgment.

b. You just know. It may come as a surprise, but
it's an acknowledgement.

c. You just know. There's not much of a surprise.
It's more of an acknowledgment.

C Share your ideas with your classmates.

1. Which voice do you remember most? What did that person say?

2. Gwen says you have to "become friends before you can become lovers."
Do you agree?

Listening Highlight

「一目ぼれ」について聞かれたら、少し照れ臭く感じる人もかもしれません。一方こ
のインタビューで、彼らは"Absolutely"、"Absolutely not"、"I do believe..."など
の言葉を用いてはっきりと自分の考えを述べていることに気づくでしょう。Gwen
の使っていたhave got toという表現にも注目です。これはhave toとほぼ同じ意
味で、よりカジュアルなhave got toは、日常会話で頻繁に耳にします。また、you've got toを、早口で
you've gotta（「ガッタ」のように発音される）と言うこともあります。

Chapter 8
Oswego, New York

ニューヨーク州最大の都市ニューヨークから車で5時間程走ると、オンタリオ湖沿岸の街、オスウィーゴに到着します。海のように広く、四季折々の変化を見せるオンタリオ湖は古くから地元の人々に愛されてきました。オンタリオとは、ネイティブ・アメリカンのイロコイ部族の言葉で「美しい湖」を意味すると言われています。アメリカというとニューヨークやロサンゼルスなどの大都市を思い浮かべますが、アメリカ全土には "small town" も数多く存在します。そのうちの1つ、オスウィーゴではどんな人々の営みに出会えるでしょうか。

Warm-up

Work in pairs and answer the questions.

1. Locate Oswego on the map on page 8.
2. Do you come from a small town or a big city?
3. What is your hometown famous for?

Match each word or phrase with the Japanese.

1. oneness   [   ]
2. bonfire   [   ]
3. launch   [   ]
4. unsupervised   [   ]

5. title   [   ]
6. compliment   [   ]
7. let go of   [   ]
8. burst into tears [   ]

a. 焚き火	**b.** 肩書き	**c.** ～を手放す	**d.** お世辞
e. 泣き出す	**f.** 一体感	**g.** 保護者なしで	**h.** 発射する

Part 1 Getting to Know the Place online video

Watch the video and answer the following questions about Oswego.

1 What is the largest celebration of the year in Oswego called?

a. Lakefest

b. Snowfest

c. Harborfest

2 Lake Ontario is...

a. not one of the Great Lakes.

b. the smallest of the Great Lakes.

c. the largest of the Great Lakes.

3 Who does Dom say is allowed to play at Donabella Rink?

a. 10- to 15-year-olds

b. Anyone

c. People who sign up

4 What did Mike NOT say he did as a 9-year-old?

a. Launch rockets

b. Have water balloon fights

c. Go swimming in the lake

Part 2 Learning More

(online / video)

Watch the video about the iconic diner in Oswego, Rudy's Lakeside Diner, and then complete the following notes.

Basic facts

- An Oswego ¹_____ = known throughout the country
- Has been serving ²_____ food since ³_____
  → The menu includes Texas ⁴_____ Sauce, the ⁵_____ chowder, and so on.

CEO, Jason

- Despite being a CEO, he considers himself as a ⁶_____.
- *Why do people love Rudy's?*
  "We try to maintain the same appearance, the same ⁷_____, and the same ⁸_____ experience as a long time ago."
- *Won't you make it a franchise?*
  "Rudy's is our ⁹_____ of our family. We don't want to allow someone else to influence or change what we believe."

Former CEO, Carol

- She was the ¹⁰_____ and CEO for more than ¹¹_____ years.
- Many of her ¹²_____ come back and tell her how much her ¹³_____ helped them.

Rudy's strength as a family business

- Jason thinks customers are ¹⁴_____ of Rudy's family.

Read the passage and answer the following questions.

Oswego: A Refuge for the Persecuted

During World War II, millions of people lost their homes across Europe. Four million Jews had already been killed by the Nazis by the time the
5 United States started helping them by bringing some refugees to America in 1943. As fate would have it, that camp would be in Oswego, NY.

Safe Haven Holocaust Refugee Shelter Museum

Over three thousand people applied for one thousand places. They came from 18
10 European countries and were invited by President Roosevelt to remain as guests until the war was over. Each person had to sign a legal document promising to return at the end of the fighting in Europe.

After a 2-week boat ride across the Atlantic in cramped quarters and stifling heat, they were greeted by the Statue of Liberty in New York Harbor. But were
15 they free? After a daylong train up to Oswego they arrived at the site of what would be their new home for the next 18 months. It was surrounded by a fence with barbed wire that looked somewhat similar to what they had escaped. But they were safe and had plenty of food. Local people would come and bring gifts. Communication was difficult because few of the refugees in the camp spoke English.

20 When the war ended, it was time to send them back. This, however, would be impractical, if not impossible. Europe was a wasteland and these people had nothing left in the countries they had run from. Suddenly, in a surprise move, Joseph Smart the director of the camp resigned and started a petition to gain support for allowing the refugees to stay. It was a long road, but in the end, he
25 succeeded.

History has proven, again and again, that there are times when people just need a helping hand. America could have done more, but Oswego had a small role in lifting these people up when they needed it most.

Notes persecute「迫害する」 cramped quarter「窮屈な空間」 stifling「息の詰まるような」
barbed「尖った、とげのある」 petition「嘆願」

56

A Answer if the following statements are true (T) or false (F).

1. The refugees were invited by the President of the United States. [T / F]

2. Very few refugees spoke English. [T / F]

3. All the refugees returned to Europe after the war. [T / F]

B Answer the following questions.

1. In Oswego, what were the conditions like for the refugees?

_____

2. What did Joseph Smart do after he resigned as director of the camp?

_____

郊外の小さな街のアメリカンライフ

　comfortable, cozy, friendly...といった言葉が似合う小さな街オスウィーゴ。この街で

A typical backyard in Oswego

は、まさに日本人がイメージする平均的なアメリカンライフをかいま見ることができます。そして人々の生活に欠かせないものがバックヤード（裏庭）なのです。

　アメリカ郊外の平均的な住宅には、フロントヤード（前庭）とバックヤード（裏庭）があります。フロントヤードは、家の玄関前の芝生の庭で、私的な空間でありながら公的な空間でもあります。そのためフロントヤードは、その住宅街の全体の風景と調和していることが求められます。一方バックヤードは、家族の私的な空間です。子育て中の家庭では、子ども達が広々とした芝生の庭でキャッチボールをしたり、飛び回って遊ぶことができます。ブランコや滑り台、ベンチやプールなどがある家もあります。そこは近所や親しい友人を招いてバーベキューやパーティーを開いたり、時には住宅の外壁を使って映画の上映会を開いたりする場所でもあり、それがまさにアメリカ人のおもてなしなのです。

　オスウィーゴの街ではのんびりとした郊外の暮らしが楽しめますが、地元密着の食堂（ダイナー）や映画館、大学などの施設も一通り揃っており、1861年からの歴史を持つニューヨーク州立大学のオスウィーゴ校には、現在約8,000人の学生が通っています。同校の前身であるオスウィーゴ師範学校には、かつて文部省派遣留学生として学んだ日本人がいました。旧会津藩士の息子であった高嶺秀夫（1854-1910）です。スイスの教育学者ペスタロッチの教育主義に基づく開発教授法を学び、暗記中心の授業ではなく、児童の自発性を重視する教育法を日本に広めることによって、明治期の教育改革に大きな役割を果たしました。

American Voices #8

What is your typical diet?
Before you watch the video,
share your ideas with your partner.

online / video
online / audio

DL 17   CD 17

A Who said it? Match the person with what was said.

1 [   ]   2 [   ]   3 [   ]

a. You have to eat everything with chili. And I love spicy food.

b. I'm actually a vegan. I love using fruits and leafy greens.

c. We have two small children. We try to limit our intake of fast food and unhealthy foods.

B Watch the video again. Which of the following did Steve say?

a. As a child, I liked eating meat.

b. I learned how much better eating plants is for the environment.

c. Humans are essentially animal eaters, but that is changing these days.

C Share your ideas with your classmates.

1. Two of the voices are vegans. Could you imagine being vegan?

2. Mercedez says, "My rule is 'try everything twice.'" Do you have this rule? Is there anything you won't eat?

Listening Highlight

どの人も食へのこだわりを持っていることがうかがえます。幼い子どもを持つ男性は、食事は "a big part of making sure that they grow up healthy" と述べており、子どもの健やかな成長を確実にするために日常の食事は重要で、不健康なものは食べないと語っています。メキシコ文化の影響を色濃く受けているニューメキシコ州に住む男性は、食べ物も文化や歴史、宗教と同様で、人生の一部であると述べています。ニューメキシコでは青唐辛子が欠かせない食材で、マクドナルドのハンバーガーにも入っています。

Chapter 9

Austin, Texas

オースティンは、メキシコと国境を接するアメリカ南西部テキサス州の州都です。以前、テキサス州の主な産業は綿花の栽培と牧畜でしたが、20世紀初頭に油田が発見されて以来、石油産業を軸に急速な発展を遂げることになります。1990年代に入ると州都オースティンでIT産業が発展。Dellをはじめとする大企業のほか多くのベンチャー企業が拠点を置き、注目を集めています。一方で豊かな自然にも恵まれ、カヤックやカヌー、都市部の生息数としては世界最大と言われるコウモリも観光名物です。

Warm-up

Work in pairs and answer the questions.

1. Locate Austin on the map on page 8.
2. What are your images of Texas?
3. Do you have any friends that are unique? How so?

Vocabulary Preview

Match each word or phrase with the Japanese.

1. republic   [   ]
2. reservoir   [   ]
3. dusk   [   ]
4. pest   [   ]

5. venue   [   ]
6. coin   [   ]
7. overlook   [   ]
8. conservative [   ]

| a. 夕暮れ時 | b. 新語を造る | c. 会場 | d. 保守的な |
| e. 貯水池 | f. 見過ごす | g. 害虫 | h. 共和国 |

Part 1 Getting to Know the Place

online video

Watch the video and answer the following questions about Austin.

1 What does the star on the Texas flag symbolize?

  a. Loyalty
  b. Unity
  c. Liberty

2 What is one month you can surely see the bats?

  a. January
  b. April
  c. July

3 How many people visit Barton Springs Pool annually?

  a. 80,000
  b. 800,000
  c. 180,000

4 What does Todd NOT say you can do on South Congress?

a. Shop for vintage clothes

b. Bicycle on a trail

c. Go see live music

 Part 2 Learning More

(online video)

Watch the video about what the three people like about living in Austin, and then complete the following notes.

Love for Austin

- There's plenty of ¹_____ all day every day.
- It is the ²_____ music capital of the world.
  ➡ Music going on all the time, and a lot of ³_____ energy

- They say "Keep ⁴_____ ⁵_____."
- It's a very ⁶_____ place.
- People want to ⁷_____ and ⁸_____.

- I love the immense amount of ⁹_____ the people hold.
- The stereotypical Texan = a very ¹⁰_____ and backwoods mentality
  ➡ In reality, it's more about ¹¹_____ pride and values, taking pride in your ¹²_____. There's a work ¹³_____ that goes along with it.

- Being "weird" is widely ¹⁴_____.
- I like to do typewriter ¹⁵_____.
  ➡ People walk up to me and tell me about their ¹⁶_____, and I'll write a poem for them.

Read the passage and answer the following questions.

Keep Austin Weird

America does not have the same way of thinking as Japan in regard to standing out. While it is often said in Japan that a nail that sticks up will be hammered down, Americans are more likely
5 to be attracted. This also holds true for places. While "weird" might be an unwanted description for most, Austin wears it with pride.

The Cathedral of Junk in Austin

Austin had always been known as a cool town, not very expensive and full of creative people. After
10 a sudden tech boom in the 90s, housing prices skyrocketed, and chain stores could not wait to move in. People wanted to support local businesses, encourage creativity of artists and musicians, and just stop the growth that could take away from what made Austin special in the first place. The idea to counter
15 all of this came in the phrase, "Keep Austin Weird."

Although Austin has been one of the fastest growing cities in America for the past 10 years, it still has plenty of weirdness and creativity. There is a Cathedral of Junk: the name says it all. Austinites believe the taco can also be breakfast food! There is no shortage of taco restaurants with breakfast tacos on the menu.

20 As for creative festivals, Austin has two of the best. The first is the Austin City Limits Music Festival that started in 2002 as a weekend celebration. Since 2013, it has been held over two weekends and is attended by around 450,000 people. The second is the SXSW (South by Southwest) festival. It began in 1987 as a one-day music event and now lasts 10 days. The festival includes an interactive track, a music
25 track, and, perhaps the most famous, a film track.

So, if you need to add a little weirdness and creativity to your life, come meet some Austinites over a breakfast taco. I'm sure you will leave more than a little inspired.

Notes tech boom「ハイテクバブル、ITバブル」　skyrocket「急騰する」　counter「立ち向かう」
track「(各セッションの) カテゴリー、ジャンル」

A Answer if the following statements are true (T) or false (F).

1. Austin housing prices rose in the 90s. [T / F]

2. People eat tacos for breakfast in Austin. [T / F]

3. Austin City Limits is a film festival. [T / F]

B Answer the following questions.

1. What are three things the "Keep Austin Weird" movement supports?

   _____

2. What are two festivals held in Austin?

   _____

テキサンの誇りと"Weird"な街作り

　人口、面積共に全米第2位のテキサス州は、カウボーイの街からハイテク産業の街へと急変したその歴史と独自性が特徴です。メキシコ領であったテキサス周辺は、テキサス革命（1835-1836）を経て、テキサス共和国（1836-1845）として独立しました。その首都オースティンの名は、独立を主導し、「テキサスの父」として知られるスティーブン・オースティンに由来しています。共和国は9年後にアメリカ合衆国に併合されましたが、ローンスター（一つ星）が描かれるその国旗は、今でも州旗に引き継がれ、テキサン（Texan）の誇りを象徴しています。

　オースティンは、保守的だと言われるテキサス州の他の都市とは異なり、自由な空気や芸術、世界的なライブ音楽の中心地でもあります。毎年サウス・バイ・サウスウエスト（SXSW）と呼ばれる世界最大規模の音楽祭、映画祭等を含むイベントも、オースティンで開催されます。近年はインターネット関連の新技術や独創的なアイデアを持つ起業家達の交流の場ともなっており、毎年規模を拡大しています。また、オースティンは200近くのライブハウスを有するとも言われ、街のあちこちでインディーズ音楽をはじめとした様々な音楽の生演奏を聞くことができます。街でよく見かける"Keep Austin Weird"という言葉は、最先端技術の追求と同時に、地元に根付いた産業や独自の風土をしたたかに守っていく、オースティンの人々の心意気を示しているのかもしれません。

Sign at Austin-Bergstrom International Airport

What makes you most proud of your country?
Before you watch the video, share your ideas
with your partner.

online / video
online / audio

DL 19   CD 19

A Who said it? Match the person with what was said.

 **1** [   ]    **2** [   ]    **3** [   ]

a. We rally together to help others. We want to help people rise to the top.

b. I'm really proud of the diversity that we have here.

c. We've also had great success in technology and industry.

B Watch the video again. Which of the following did Jack say?

a. I am proud of our founding fathers and immigrants.

b. I am proud of the guidelines in our constitution, things like freedom of speech and monarchism.

c. I am proud of the guidelines in our constitution, things like free speech and representative government.

C Share your ideas with your classmates.

1. Do you feel there are more opportunities for the younger generation?

2. Mercedez said, "I have faith in my fellow Americans, whether they know me or not, to hopefully stand up for me, if they see me being mistreated." Would you help a stranger?

Listening Highlight

アメリカ人の誇りとして、多様な移民の国の国民であること、人に対して親切であるといったコメントがあります。日本人も親切だと言われています。しかし日本には「世間」と「社会」があり、日本人は自分の属する「世間」の人々には親切で、自分と無関係な「社会」の人々には無関心である傾向があります。Mercedezが "Americans are willing to stand up for each other." と述べているように、アメリカには「世間」はなく、アメリカ人は、知っている人とも知らない人とも分け隔てなく接するのです。

Saint Jo, Texas

アメリカ南西部テキサス州の北部にある小さな町セント・ジョー。日本語にも翻訳されている『赤い河の谷間』という歌で知られるレッド川流域の、緑に囲まれたなだらかな丘にあります。まるで西部劇の舞台のようなこの町には、カウボーイハットにジーンズ、ブーツ姿がよく似合います。通りを歩けば、Howdy!（HelloやHow do you do?を意味するテキサス式の挨拶）と声をかけられるかもしれません。その時は、ぜひ笑顔でHowdy!と返してみましょう。

Warm-up

Work in pairs and answer the questions.

1. Locate Saint Jo on the map on page 8.
2. What images do you have of cowboys? What do they do?
3. Have you ever been to a farm or a ranch? Have you ever ridden a horse?

Match each word or phrase with the Japanese.

1. unmatched   [   ]   5. equine   [   ]
2. saloon   [   ]   6. herd   [   ]
3. cattle   [   ]   7. grace   [   ]
4. originate in   [   ]   8. exhausted   [   ]

| a. 畜牛 | b. 馬の | c. 疲弊した | d. 酒場、食堂 |
| e. 気品 | f. 比類ない | g. 群れ | h. 〜に由来する |

Part 1 Getting to Know the Place online video

Watch the video and answer the following questions about Saint Jo.

① What is the population of Saint Jo?

a. 1,043

b. 14,300

c. 143,000

② How long does Mike work on each pair of boots?

a. About a year

b. About 40 hours

c. About 2 weeks

③ What does Donna identify with being a Texan?

a. Friendliness

b. Isolation

c. Strength

④ Randy says, in Texas, he will be greeted by a smile...

a. only by those who know him.

b. only if they hate him.

c. even if they don't know him.

Part 2   Learning More   (online / video)

Watch the video describing a day at Four Winds Ranch, and then fill in the blanks.

A typical Day at Four Winds Ranch

What is "currying"?

● This is Carrie.
● She is the equine ^{1}_____ of the ranch.

● She is currying the horse.
● "Curry" means to ^{2}_____ and
  ^{3}_____ the horse.
  ➡ Increases ^{4}_____ and
  the horses become ^{5}_____
  to the person who does it.

What is "herd work"?

● Cows like to ^{6}_____ in the herd.
● Herd work = ^{7}_____ one from the herd
● *Why?*: Necessary when one is sold or needs
  ^{8}_____ or ^{9}_____.
● Today it's a ^{10}_____ sport.
  ➡ A judge looks at how ^{11}_____ the horse
     can work the herd.
● This is a very ^{12}_____ sport.

Read the passage and answer the following questions.

Saint Jo: The Original Cowboy

The American Cowboy embodied true American values such as independence and adventure. He answered to no one and controlled his own fate. But how much of this is fact and how much is fiction? If
5　we take a closer look at the history of the cowboy, you might be surprised by the answer.

First, we should understand the cowboy did not originate in America. Most of the tools of the cowboy come directly from Northern Mexico. Even words like *lariat*, the rope cowboys
10　use, come directly from Spanish. The American cowboy evolved over time and added new gear, such as the cowboy boot, but essentially did the same job as the Mexicans and their European predecessors.

Cowboy statue in Dallas, Texas

The job of the cowboy was simply to move cattle from the ranch to the market. It was hard work that was often dangerous. Cowboys had to live outside for long
15　periods of time and protect themselves and their cattle from robbers, rattlesnakes and even mountain lions. Native Americans weren't too happy with the gun slinging intruders either. The truth is that cowboys made little money and usually died at a young age.

How then did the image of the cowboy become so glamorous? We have fiction to
20　thank for that. While the cowboy era was relatively brief, lasting from 1865-1890, movies and books about cowboys are still popular today. Writers gave cowboys a code that may or may not have existed in real life. The code states, in part, that cowboys were kind to women and children, but ruthless with their enemies. Being a free-spirit, he might challenge an unfair law to protect some unfortunate. He was
25　always calm, cool, and handsome.

Movies are magic and the cowboy represents America like no other. Does it matter that most of the images are not real? Probably not. Every country needs a myth and those myths need to be better than reality.

Notes　gear「道具」　predecessor「先にあったもの、先祖」　rattlesnake「ガラガラヘビ」　mountain lion「アメリカライオン、クーガー」　sling「(肩に) つるす」　code「符号、イメージ」　ruthless「無慈悲な」

A Answer if the following statements are true (T) or false (F).

1. The first cowboys came from America. [T / F]

2. The cowboy boot originated in America. [T / F]

3. The cowboy code may not have been real. [T / F]

B Answer the following questions.

1. What was the primary job of the cowboy?

_____

2. Name three things in the "cowboy code."

_____

American Eyes

カウボーイのオアシス ―セント・ジョー

　　テキサスといえば、カウボーイを思い浮かべる人も多いことでしょう。19世紀後半、もともとヘッド・オブ・エルムという地名で知られていたセント・ジョーは、商業の中心地でした。南北戦争後の畜牛需要の急激な高まりにより、カウボーイと家畜運送者達は、チザム・トレイル（Chisholm Trail）と呼ばれた道を通って、テキサスの農場からカンザスの市場へ牛を運びました。その労働は過酷なもので、何日も続く遠征中にいなくなってしまう牛たちもいたと言います。セント・ジョーは、そんなカウボーイ達にとって旅の疲れを癒す場でした。映像に登場するストーンウォール・サルーンもその1つで、チザム・トレイルを移動したカウボーイ達の宿としての役割を果たしました。

　　19世紀末に鉄道が普及し、チザム・トレイルはその役割を終えましたが、この道を通って約35,000人のカウボーイ達が延べ600万～1,000万頭にものぼる牛を運んだと言われ、世界で最大規模の家畜の移動であったとされています。こうして、カウボーイのイメージが世界に広まりました。

　　カウボーイと言えば、西部劇の登場人物が話すテキサス英語（Texan English）を思い起こす人も多いでしょう。南部訛りの母音を伸ばした話し方や、スラングでも耳にする、am notをain'tとする言い方などが特徴です。（例：This ain't my first rodeo!「前にやったことあるよ！」）

Sign of a cowboy church in Texas

American Voices #10

What is your fashion sense?
Before you watch the video,
share your ideas with your partner.

online / video
online / audio

 DL 21 CD 21

A Who said it? Match the person with what was said.

1 [   ]   2 [   ]   3 [   ]

a. Be subtle with your outfits.

b. If I come to your wedding, I'm wearing 501 jeans.

c. As you can see, I love black. It's slimming.

B Watch the video again. Which of the following did John say?

a. Some dress plainly. And they dress for efficiency.

b. Some dress seriously. And they dress for business.

c. I like Mark Zuckerberg as a businessperson, but I don't like the way he dresses.

C Share your ideas with your classmates.

1. How would you feel about wearing the same thing every day?

2. Yobi says, "I got on our good friend, YouTube, and learned everything." What do you learn from YouTube?

Listening Highlight

日本語のカタカナ発音とは異なる英語の発音には気付きましたか。necklace の lace [leis] は飾りのレースのことで、「ネックレス」ではなく、「ネックレイス」に近い発音です。ビーチサンダルは和製英語で、英語では flip-flops です。サンダルで歩くときにパタパタ鳴る音を flip-flop と表すので、そのままサンダルの名前になったそうです。
特定のブランド名に言及していた人もいました。Levi's 501 は、世界のジーンズの原型です。6 歳からずっとはき続けているという彼のこだわりが伝わってきますね。

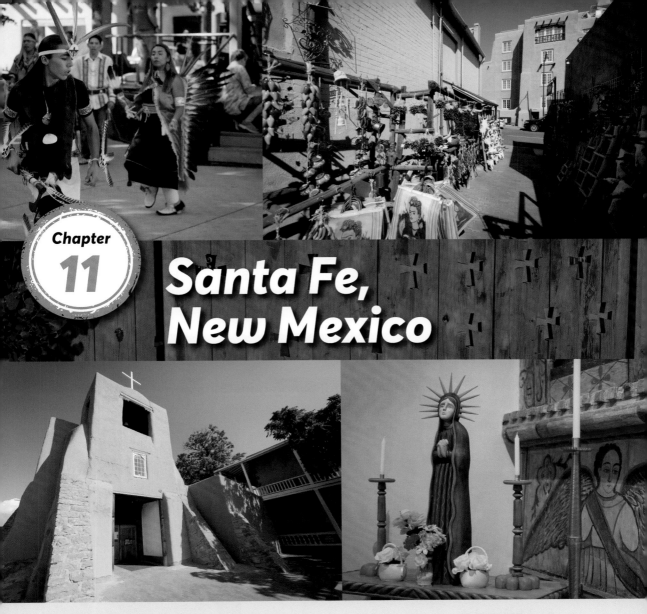

Chapter 11

Santa Fe, New Mexico

歴史と芸術の街サンタフェは、アメリカ南西部のニューメキシコ州北部、ロッキー山脈の南端にあります。遠い昔にタイムスリップしたかのようなアドビ建築の美しい街並みと、アメリカ先住民やスペイン、メキシコ文化の融合は、世界中から訪れる観光客を魅了しています。100年近い歴史を誇るサンタフェ・インディアン・マーケットでは、220以上の部族のアーティストによる作品や、伝統的な音楽と踊りのパフォーマンスが必見です。

Warm-up

Work in pairs and answer the questions.

1. Locate Santa Fe on the map on page 8.
2. What images do you have of Native Americans?
3. Are all traditions important to follow? Why or why not?

Vocabulary Preview

Match each word or phrase with the Japanese.

1. existing   [   ]   5. federally   [   ]
2. mixture   [   ]   6. penetrate   [   ]
3. cliff   [   ]   7. disheartening   [   ]
4. preserve   [   ]   8. tribe   [   ]

a. 保存する	**b.** がっかりさせる	**c.** 現存する	**d.** しみ込む
e. 崖	**f.** 融合	**g.** 部族	**h.** 連邦政府によって

Part 1   Getting to Know the Place

online video

Watch the video and answer the following questions about Santa Fe.

1 Who founded Santa Fe in 1610?

   a. The French
   b. The Spanish
   c. The Americans

2 What is traditional adobe made of?

   a. Mud and straw
   b. Concrete and steel
   c. Clay and brick

3 What does Hector say about Santa Fe?

   a. It's really just like Mexico.
   b. It's not the USA at all.
   c. It has its own identity.

4 When is the Indian Market?

   a. The third week each month

   b. The third week in August

   c. The third weekend of the year

Part **2**   **Learning More**   (online / video)

Watch the video about the Native American culture: their past and present. Next, complete the following notes.

Puye Cliffs = The Pueblo people lived from ^{1}_____ AD to 1500 AD.

● The cliffs were over a ^{2}_____ long, and had at least ^{3}_____ rooms.

● Once a home to around ^{4}_____ Pueblo Indians
 ➡ They farmed and ^{5}_____.

● The rooms are small and the inside is ^{6}_____.

● They are ^{7}_____ and seem to fall apart, but do not.

Ohkay Owingeh people = one of 19 federally recognized Pueblos

▶**David**

● The Ohkay Owingeh people are trying to ^{8}_____ their traditions.

● Preparing a ^{9}_____ hide

  (1) Cook and blend pork ^{10}_____ to make a paste

  (2) Hang it out to ^{11}_____

  (3) Make products such as a ^{12}_____

▶**Georgina**

● Her generation fights hard to get recognized.
 ➡ There's a lot of ^{13}_____ on ^{14}_____ media,
 teaching people about Native American history.

● Native Americans come from different places, and there are so many different
 ^{15}_____.

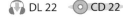

DL 22　　CD 22

Read the passage and answer the following questions.

Preserving the Past: Santa Fe

Adobe house in Santa Fe

Every year we lose a bit of our past. Older buildings are torn down to make way for new ones. Sometimes the modern structures are imaginative,
5 but often they are not. Imagine what your city would look like if there were a law in place saying that all buildings in the center of town had to be in a certain style. Imagine Santa Fe.

10 　In 1957, the first New Mexico preservation ordinance was put in place. It stated that all the buildings in the historic center had to be in Santa Fe style. Buildings had to be in a Spanish Pueblo style, or at least, imitate the look of adobe. The result is a beautiful city with the look of a romantic past like no other.

　Adobe is made of mud and straw and is perfect in the desert climate as it keeps
15 the rooms cool during the day and warm at night. It is organic, originally only in earth tones with rounded corners. Upkeep, however, is time consuming and costly and so many of the "historic" buildings are actually in a faux-adobe style. They look like adobe but actually have concrete mixes under what appears to be mud. This doesn't take away from the experience of the average tourist, though. Santa Fe still
20 looks like a dreamland.

　Adobe colors can be pink, blue, or a range of other colors now, but it can be tough designing a new house in the historic district because all designs have to be approved by a city board. Some believe the uniformity is not only historically inaccurate, but also stifles creativity. If you have a chance to visit Santa Fe, would you love the
25 uniformity, or would you find the laws stifling for those who dream of creating something new?

Notes　in place「(法律などが)実施されて」　ordinance「条例」　earth tone「アースカラー」　upkeep「維持、保持」
faux-「見せかけの、～を模した」　stifle「抑制する、鎮圧する」

74

A Answer if the following statements are true (T) or false (F).

1. All the buildings in New Mexico have to be in Santa Fe style.　　[T / F]

2. Some adobe houses today use different colors with pointed corners.

　　　　　　　　　　　　　　　　　　　　　　　　　　　　　[T / F]

3. New building designs must be approved by a city board.　　[T / F]

B Answer the following questions.

1. Why are some buildings in Santa Fe not real adobe?

_____

2. Why are some people against the preservation ordinance?

_____

伝統と新しさの融合
―個性光るアートと先住民の暮らし

　　紀元前から先住民が居住していたサンタフェ周辺は、スペインやメキシコ、アメリカなど、様々な国の支配を受けました。サンタフェは、1610年にスペイン植民地政府の中枢として総督邸が建設されたことにより、アメリカ最古の州都としても知られています。

　1880年、南西部にサンタフェ鉄道が開通すると、プエブロ族やナバホ族などの工芸品が観光の呼び物に利用されました。その後20世紀初頭にかけて芸術の街へと発展し、1950年代以降の公民権運動の活発化、1960～70年代のインディアン復権運動が追い風となり、1962年には、アメリカ先住民のための全米唯一の芸術専門教育機関であるアメリカン・インディアン・アーツ研究所が設置されました。現在、市内にあるギャラリーや美術商の数は200を超え、サンタ

Piece of art seen on Canyon Road

フェは全米屈指のアートの街でもあります。中でも多くのギャラリーが密集するキャニオン・ロードという通りでは、カラフルなネイティブ・アメリカンの工芸品から現代美術まで、多様で個性溢れるアート作品に触れることができるでしょう。

　サンタフェを含むニューメキシコ州の先住民は、伝統を受け継ぎながら新しい文化も柔軟に受け入れていますが、それぞれのアイデンティティをとても大切にしています。映像ではネイティブ・アメリカンの部族の1つ「オーケイオウェンゲ」(Ohkay Owingeh：プエブロ族の部族) 出身のジョージナという女性が、ネイティブ・アメリカンの各部族における独立性や独自性について語っています。実際、現在アメリカ政府に認定されている先住民の部族の数は600近くにのぼり、彼らの肌の色や言葉、生活様式は多岐にわたります。こうしたことから、黒髪や羽根飾りといった「インディアン」像は、メディアによって強調されたステレオタイプであることに気づかされるのではないでしょうか。

American Voices #11

Let's meet two artists based in Santa Fe: Andres Martinez, and Kata Bennet.

online / video
online / audio

🎧 DL 23 ⦿ CD 23

A **Watch Andres' interview and put T (True) or F (False) in the brackets for each statement.**

1. He lived in California before returning to New Mexico.
( )

2. He did not want his children to lose their culture. ( )

3. His brothers and sister live near his house. ( )

B **Which of the following did Kata mention about her job and her adobe house?**

❶ *I've found what I want to do with the rest of my life, which is...*

a. building adobes   b. relocating adobes
c. restoring adobes

❷ *My adobe house...*

a. stays warm throughout the year.
b. is a little larger than 2,000 square feet.
c. has 10 feet of dirt on the roof.

C **Share your ideas with your classmates.**

1. What kind of house would you like to live in? How would you design your house?

2. Kata says, "I think I've really found what I want to do with the rest of my life…" Do you have any ideas what you want to do with the rest of your life?

Listening Highlight

Andresも述べているように、ネイティブ・アメリカンの言語や文化、宗教などが加速度的に消滅しています。自分の言語を捨てて、アメリカで英語を使用して生きていくべきなのかというジレンマを、多くの人々が抱えています。アドビの家の内部を案内してくれたKataは、Viga（ヴィーガ）と呼ばれる天井に渡された太い丸太の梁や、泥で作られたアート作品などを紹介し、伝統的なアドビ建築のあり方を後世に伝えようと活動しています。

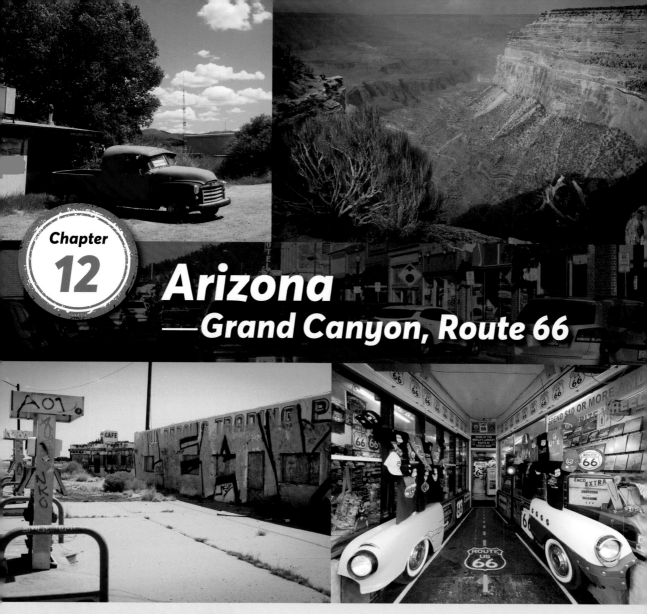

Chapter 12

Arizona
—Grand Canyon, Route 66

想像を絶するほどの広大な峡谷グランド・キャニオン。自然の偉大さを実感させられます。グランド・キャニオン国立公園は千葉県とほぼ同じ大きさで、アメリカ最古の国立公園に指定されています。アメリカ南西部に位置するアリゾナ州の北部にあり、コロラド川の浸食作用によって何億年もの歳月をかけて作られました。グランド・キャニオンから100キロほど車で下ると、ピクサー映画『カーズ』(2006) にも登場するような、ルート66沿いのノスタルジックな街並みを堪能することができます。

Warm-up

Work in pairs and answer the questions.

1. Locate the Grand Canyon on the map on page 8.
2. Have you ever been to a National Park? Where was it?
3. What do you think is the best way to travel: cars or trains?

Match each word or phrase with the Japanese.

1. edge   [   ]   5. highway   [   ]
2. intermingle   [   ]   6. trading post   [   ]
3. frustrating   [   ]   7. ruins   [   ]
4. cricket   [   ]   8. souvenir   [   ]

a. 混ざり合う	**b.** お土産	**c.** 高速道路	**d.** 廃墟
e. 縁、へり	**f.** コオロギ	**g.** 交易所	**h.** イライラする

Part 1 Getting to Know the Place

online video

Watch the video and answer the following questions about Arizona.

1. What year did the Grand Canyon become a National Park?

   a. 1903
   b. 1906
   c. 1919

2. What does Mercedez say about Williams?

   a. The town used to be smaller.
   b. It is not very international.
   c. It is small but international.

3. Brian says most people visit Williams for...

   a. the logging and mining.
   b. the Grand Canyon.
   c. the car shows.

4 What does the Grand Canyon Railway also protect?

a. The environment

b. The scenery

c. The tourist population

Part 2 Learning More

(online / video)

Watch the video about Route 66 and towns along it, and then complete the following notes.

Route 66 = one of the ^{1}_____ highways in the US

- *Period*   Began in ^{2}_____ / Officially ended in ^{3}_____
- *Distance*   Originally ran ^{4}_____ km
  ➡ From Chicago, ^{5}_____ through Missouri, Kansas, Oklahoma, ^{6}_____,
     New Mexico and Arizona ➡ Finish in Santa Monica, ^{7}_____
- Parts of it are known as ^{8}_____ Route 66.
  ➡ We can see the ^{9}_____ of abandoned trading posts and towns.

Towns along Route 66

▶ **Flagstaff**

Hi, my name is Clementine. I'm from Flagstaff. Here, you get to meet so many people from many ^{10}_____ places.

▶ **Williams**

Williams reminds people of the times when the highways were smaller, and the ^{11}_____ were ^{12}_____.

  ➡ *Advice*: Stay in a ^{13}_____ and walk to one of the ^{14}_____.
     There are plenty of ^{15}_____ shops featuring Route 66.

 online audio

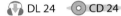 DL 24 CD 24

Read the passage and answer the following questions.

Picture Perfect Arizona

Things look better from a distance as many postcards show. It is not uncommon for crowds and litter to make a landmark less than expected. This has been true for
5 years, but today things have fundamentally changed.

Tourists visiting Grand Canyon National Park

A tourist is one type of visitor who just wants to see and take photos of famous places. For example, most of the 5.5 million visitors per year who visit the Grand
10 Canyon in Arizona stay little more than half an hour, and do little more than take selfies before going shopping and returning to their hotel. A second type of visitor, the traveler, wants to experience what a place has to offer. As opposed to the tourist, the experiential traveler to the Grand Canyon will want to hike some of the 640 km of trails. While it takes four to six hours to get down to the
15 Colorado River, breathtaking views can be seen every minute of the way.

The advent of cell phones and social media has given rise to a third category of visitor who is now everywhere. They are the people in search of the perfect selfie, and they have transformed scenic, yet sparsely populated, places. For example, Horseshoe Bend, in a town called Page, Arizona, used to get a few thousand
20 visitors a year until Instagram started in 2010. That year, with its newly found fame, 100,000 people visited, and by 2015, the number climbed to 750,000. These days, 2 million are expected every year. The town has only 7,000 residents and they can't handle the concerns that come with so many people passing through.

With visitors come jobs and money for improving local communities. Sudden
25 increases in visitors, however, can strain the resources those communities have to preserve the landmark for future visitors. Only time will tell if access to famous landmarks will be restricted.

Notes litter「ポイ捨てゴミ」 Colorado River「コロラド川（アメリカ南西部を流れる全長2,330kmの川。グランドキャニオンの大峡谷はこの川の侵食でもたらされた）」 advent「出現」 sparsely populated「人口の少ない」 Horseshoe Bend「ホースシュー・ベンド（アリゾナ州のペイジという町にある、コロラド川が作り出した馬蹄のような形をした絶景スポット）」 strain「負担をかける」

A **Answer if the following statements are true (T) or false (F).**

1. Most visitors to the Grand Canyon go hiking for hours. [T / F]

2. The town of Page has a population of 7,000. [T / F]

3. People living near Horseshoe Bend are concerned with the increase
   in visitors. [T / F]

B **Answer the following questions.**

1. Describe three types of people who travel.

   _____

2. What seems to have caused the increase in visitors at Horseshoe Bend?

   _____

American Eyes

「古き良きアメリカ」を体現するルート66

　イリノイ州シカゴとカリフォルニア州サンタモニカを結ぶ全長3,940kmの旧国道ルート66は、1926年以来、アメリカ南西部の発展に貢献したアメリカ初の大陸横断道路でした。「マザー・ロード」として親しまれたルート66は、車文化やファーストフード、モーテルを普及させ、夢を求めて旅する人々や冒険家で賑わいました。1984年に高速道路が新設されるまでは、まさにアメリカン・ドリームの象徴だったのです。しかし、高速道路によって利用者が激減し、1985年に廃道になりました。映画『カーズ』にも描かれているように、かつて賑わった町は廃墟となりました。しかしその後ルート66を復活させようという動きが高まります。ルート66沿いの街で理髪店を営んでいたある男性が、友人達と協力し、1987年に非営利団体Historic Route 66 Association of Arizonaを立ち上げ、ルート66の保護・宣伝活動に勤しみました。こうした努力の結果、現在は一部の区間が「ヒストリック・ルート66」として、国指定景観街道に指定されています。

Historic Route 66 sign

　ルート66は、数多くの小説や映画、ドラマの中にも登場します。スタインベックの小説『怒りの葡萄』(1939) では、貧困に苦しむ主人公とその家族が新天地カリフォルニアを目指した道であり、映画『イージー・ライダー』(1969) では、自由を追い求める若者が、ハーレーダビッドソンでルート66を走る様子が描かれました。

　ルート66の大半は、アメリカ先住民部族の居留地を通る道でもあり、現在でも多くの先住民がその沿道で暮らしています。ルート66周辺のグランド・キャニオンやモニュメント・バレーはアメリカ先住民の聖地になっており、多くの観光客が訪れています。

American Voices #12

What concerns you most about the future of your country? Before you watch the video, share your ideas with your partner.

online / video
online / audio

🎧 DL 25   ⊚ CD 25

A Who said it? Match the person with what was said.

 1 [   ]    2 [   ]    3 [   ]

a. Global warming. We don't deal with that in the ways we should.

b. We've forgotten the very notion of a complex and different sense of unity.

c. In the US, we value the individual over the collective. And there's been an erosion or doing away with a lot of those protections.

B Watch the video again. Which of the following did Evlondo say?

a. Not many people work very hard these days.

b. Millions of hard-working Americans do not have enough money to take care of their basic health needs.

c. Americans have enough food, but many of them are not healthy.

C Share your ideas with your classmates.

1. In the video, three people mention something to do with immigration. Do you think your country should allow more immigrants?

2. Lauryn says, "I think when we don't acknowledge our history, we run the chance of making the same mistakes." Do you agree with what she says? Do you think it is important to study history?

Listening Highlight

アメリカの将来への不安について、貧富の差の拡大、温暖化、基本的人権が脅かされていることなどが懸念点として挙げられています。Aletheaは、アメリカは "built off of people from all different parts of the world"「様々な地域から来た人々により建国された」国でありながら、こうした人々への寛大さが失われてきていることを指摘しています。彼女の発言から、アメリカ人であることの誇りと、現状への困惑が読み取れます。

Los Angeles 1

映画の街ハリウッド。セレブの邸宅が建ち並ぶビバリーヒルズ。アメリカ最大の日本人街リトルトーキョー。これらはいずれもカリフォルニア州のロサンゼルスにあります。アメリカ西海岸に位置するカリフォルニア州は年間を通して雨量が少なく、温暖で過ごしやすい気候が特徴です。その最大の都市であるロサンゼルス (Los Angeles) はスペイン語で「天使たち」を意味し、その名前が示す通り、スペイン、メキシコなどのヒスパニック系の民族も多く、国際色豊かな地域です。

Warm-up

Work in pairs and answer the questions.

1. Locate Los Angeles on the map on page 8.
2. Share your images of Los Angeles with a partner.
3. Do you like movies? Name your favorite movies or actors.

Vocabulary Preview

Match each word or phrase with the Japanese.

1. realty   [   ]   **5.** exclusion act   [   ]

2. make up   [   ]   **6.** round up   [   ]

3. honor   [   ]   **7.** internment camp   [   ]

4. motion picture   [   ]   **8.** heritage   [   ]

a. 映画	**b.** 遺産	**c.** 検挙する	**d.** 名誉を与える
e. 強制収容所	**f.** 排斥法	**g.** 不動産	**h.** 構成する

Part **1** Getting to Know the Place

online video

Watch the video and answer the following questions about Los Angeles.

1 What did the Hollywood sign read when it was built?

    a. Hollywood Realty

    b. Hollywoodland

    c. Holly Woodlands

2 Which category was added to the Walk of Fame in 1984?

    a. Television and Radio

    b. Motion Pictures and Music

    c. Theater and Live Performance

3 What is one star that is NOT found in the video?

    a. Jackie Chan

    b. Jaws

    c. Martin Scorsese

4 What is one thing Carl says about the vibe of
Los Angeles?

  a. It runs at a faster speed than New York.

  b. It is more relaxed than New York.

  c. You can't get away from the entertainment
industry.

 Part **2**   **Learning More**   (online / video)

**Watch the video about Little Tokyo, the largest Japanese town in the
country, and then complete the following notes.**

A brief history

- 1905~   Japanese population ¹_____ grew until ²_____.
- 1941   Population peaked at ³_____. ➡ The ⁴_____ came.
- 1942   The Japanese were taken to ⁵_____ camps.
- Today   Relatively ⁶_____ Japanese people live here.

How to enjoy Little Tokyo

▶ **A great place for shopping**
- You can buy some of the most ⁷_____ Japanese foods.
  - ➡ ⁸_____ sushi, udon, and even mochi ⁹_____ ¹⁰_____, etc.
- You can also get cool ¹¹_____.

▶ **The Nisei Week Festival**
- It started in ¹²_____ and is held in ¹³_____.
- The idea is to promote Japanese ¹⁴_____ and traditions.
- There are many things to do.
  - ➡ A ¹⁵_____ eating contest
    A parade with children, ¹⁶_____ leaders and the festival
    ¹⁷_____ of the year

Reading

online / audio

🎧 DL 26   ◉ CD 26

Read the passage and answer the following questions.

Hollywood: Upstaging New Jersey

Hollywood is the movie capital of the world. But this wasn't always the case. In fact, a series of events combined to make that happen. If any of the key moments in history

5　did not occur, people may never have heard of Hollywood and the famous song might have been "Hooray for Fort Lee, New Jersey!"

The Globe Theatre in Hollywood

The small town of Fort Lee, across the river from New York City, had good reasons to be the first movie capital. The first was Thomas Edison, the inventor

10　of motion picture equipment. His laboratory was nearby. Another reason was that talented Broadway actors were close by and could star in the new silent movies. A third reason was that Fort Lee had the Hudson River and a rock formation called the Palisades, which were perfect scenery for the movies. During its most productive time, 1908-1917, Fort Lee was home to seven major studios and made

15　over 900 films. Universal Studios started in Fort Lee.

Despite these advantages, things were not perfect. First, Edison wanted to completely control the movie industry. Second, coal was rationed during WWI, and it became increasingly difficult to heat movie studios. To get around this, the studios moved 2,700 miles away to far away Hollywood, California.

20　Hollywood had near perfect weather and did not require any heating like places on the East Coast. At that time in Hollywood, land prices were cheap, and it had desert, ocean, and mountains with snow not too far away. Movie producers could make movies that looked like virtually anywhere in the world. By the 1920s, Hollywood was the fifth largest industry in the nation.

25　All of this may never have happened if Edison had been more flexible or if war had not come when it did. It is up for debate whether the magic of Hollywood would have been as strong had the studios never moved westward.

Notes upstage「後方に追いやる、人気を奪う」 "Hooray for Hollywood"「ハリウッド万歳（映画 *Hotel Hollywood* (1973) のテーマ曲で、現在もアカデミー賞のセレモニーなどで使われる)」 Fort Lee「フォート・リー（ニュージャージー州にある人口約38,000人の街)」 the Palisades「パリセイズ（ハドソン川下流の急な崖の連なり)」 ration「供給制限する」 Universal Studio「ユニバーサル・スタジオ（ハリウッドのユニバーサルシティにある映画スタジオ兼テーマパーク)」

A **Answer if the following statements are true (T) or false (F).**

1. Broadway actors were used in early films. [T / F]
2. Thomas Edison moved from New Jersey to Hollywood with movie actors.

[T / F]
3. Universal Studios began in Hollywood. [T / F]

B **Answer the following questions.**

1. Why did it become difficult to heat movie studios in New Jersey during WWI?

_____

2. Name three reasons the studios moved to Hollywood.

_____

多様なルーツを持つ「アメリカ人」の街

　現在のロサンゼルスのある地域には、約1万年前から人類が暮らし、紀元前8000年頃からはネイティブ・アメリカンの部族が定住を始めたと言われています。1769年には、15世紀後半の新大陸発見以降植民地を拡大していたスペインがカリフォルニアを併合。その後、同様にスペインの植民地であったメキシコが1821年に独立戦争に勝利したことで、カリフォルニアはメキシコ領となりました。1848年にはメキシコがアメリカ・メキシコ戦争（米墨戦争）で敗北したため、カリフォルニアはアメリカの領土となり、現在に至ります。

　カリフォルニア州内でも、特にロサンゼルスは多種多様な民族や人種で構成されています。ヨーロッパ系に加え、ヒスパニック系は全米最大規模で、中東系、アジア系、アフリカ系、そしてネイティブ・アメリカンも多数居住しています。映像でSergioが話しているように、ロサンゼルスは、それぞれ独自のスタイルを持つ小さな村が集まった都市と言えるのです。

　ロサンゼルスは日本人とも関わりの深い街です。19世紀末、ロサンゼルス在住の日本人漁師による日本食店の開業が、リトルトーキョー発祥のきっかけとなりました。リトルトーキョーは、一時は30,000人を超えるほどの規模になりましたが、第二次世界大戦中、多くの日系人が強制収容所に入れられ、一時は消滅しました。戦後は再生し、映像で紹介されていたように様々な飲食店やイベントによって賑わいを取り戻しています。1992年に開館した全米日系人博物館では、戦前の日系人の生活の様子や強制収容所時代の遺物が展示され、彼らの歩みを後世に伝えています。

Banners greeting travelers to Los Angeles

Let's meet three performers who work in show business in Hollywood.

online audio
DL 27 · CD 27

A Watch two young performers talk and match the person with what was said.

 1 [　]
　　[　]

 2 [　]
　　[　]

- **a.** I'm more focused on film, television and film.
- **b.** Los Angeles offers the opportunity to follow your dreams.
- **c.** I wasn't ready to be cold yet because I'm from Florida.
- **d.** I love acting and love stand-up comedy.

B Now let's watch the famous actor Jay Mohr. Which of the following did Jay say?

- **a.** Many people with incredible dreams come to LA, but they realize that they're very small fish in a very large pond.
- **b.** Many people with a lot of experiences come to LA, but young performers never flourish.
- **c.** Life treats you well in LA. It's a beautiful city.

C Share your ideas with your classmates.

1. Who are your favorite actors and why?
2. Jay describes his position as "middle class in show business." If you were him, would you try to push the ceiling higher to be even more successful? Or would you be happy to be "middle class"?

Listening Highlight

ロサンゼルスのあるカリフォルニア州の英語は、アメリカ国内では標準語とされており、日本人でも比較的聞き取りやすいと言われています。映像に登場した2人の若い女性の話した方は、イントネーションに抑揚があることも聞き取りやすさの要因の1つでしょう。例えばSarahは "performing at stand-up comedy clubs, ↗ going for hikes ↘" のように、複数の例を挙げるときに並列関係がわかるように、語尾の上げ下げを意識して発音しています。

Chapter 14
Los Angeles 2

広大な自然と都市が共存するLA。若者から家族連れまで、老若男女の幅広い年齢層に人気のベニスビーチは、ロサンゼルスのダウンタウンから電車とバスでおよそ1時間の距離です。20世紀初頭にイタリアのベニスを模して造られました。ヤシの木が立ち並ぶビーチでは、サーフィンやスケートボード、サイクリングなど、いろいろな楽しみ方ができます。アーノルド・シュワルツェネッガーが通っていたことで有名なマッスルビーチは、巨大なコンクリートのバーベルが目印の野外ジムで、筋肉自慢の強者たちが、日々トレーニングに励んでいます。

Warm-up

Work in pairs and answer the questions.

1. Do you like the beach? What do you do there?
2. What is your favorite amusement park and why?
3. Would you like to work out in a gym or outside?

Vocabulary Preview

Match each word or phrase with the Japanese.

1. eccentric   [   ]
2. pier   [   ]
3. plunge   [   ]
4. cliché   [   ]

5. stunning   [   ]
6. veganism   [   ]
7. supportive   [   ]
8. edit   [   ]

| **a.** 決まり文句、ありふれた表現 | **b.** 菜食主義 | **c.** 風変わりな | **d.** ふ頭 |
| **e.** 驚くほどすばらしい | **f.** 編集する | **g.** 協力的な | **h.** 急降下 |

Part 1 Getting to Know the Place

online video

Watch the video and answer the following questions about Los Angeles.

1 When did Muscle Beach start?

   a. In the 1930s
   b. In the 1970s
   c. In the 1990s

2 What is NOT mentioned as something you can see at Venice Beach?

   a. Skateboarders
   b. Artists
   c. Musicians

3 Pacific Park is the only amusement park that is completely...

   a. free.
   b. on a pier.
   c. for adults.

4 What makes the Ferris Wheel at Pacific Park most unique?

a. It is by the ocean.

b. It is solar powered.

c. It generates wind power.

Part 2 — Learning More   (online / video)

Watch and see what people from LA like and dislike about their city. Then complete the following notes.

▶ Likes

"I can eat ¹_____ type of food from ²_____ in the world."
Types of food she had: Thai, ³_____ and Chinese
What she will have today: ⁴_____

"The weather is always ⁵_____."
➡ Sunshine and just a nice ⁶_____ at all ⁷_____
➡ There's so much ⁸_____.

"You really have the opportunity to be ⁹_____."
➡ You can find whatever ¹⁰_____ of life that suits you, whether that's veganism, or joining some sort of ¹¹_____, etc.

▶ Dislikes

"One problem that everybody gets —¹²_____ and ¹³_____."
➡ You will need a ¹⁴_____ to go anywhere.
➡ You have to think about how much ¹⁵_____ it's going to take you to go somewhere.

"The cost of living is ¹⁶_____."

"There's ¹⁷_____ everywhere."
➡ They ¹⁸_____ it out on TV, but it's everywhere.

Read the passage and answer the following questions.

LA: Innovative Food Culture

Ocean Front Walk of Venice Beach

Los Angeles has become home to one of the most vibrant food cultures in the world. While many chefs are steeped in tradition and perfect their dishes by looking at the
5 past, the LA way is to try something that has never been done.

A large number of the hot chefs are the children of immigrants. They may have grown up eating the traditional food of their parents, but being American, they
10 did not feel bound by tradition. Take Roy Choi for example, who started his food empire from a taco truck when he was just 24 years old. Roy is Korean-American, so he had the idea to make tacos filled with Korean BBQ. A decade later, he is one of the most famous chefs in America.

Social media is also a driving force behind the new food in LA. A lot of chefs
15 started using food trucks. It is a fraction of the cost of opening a restaurant and ideal because LA is so vast at over 500 square miles. The problem before was finding the right locations at the right time. Social media solved that problem because they could let users know where they would be and when. Hungry students even requested trucks at 2:00 a.m. outside their dorms when studying
20 for exams! The result was innovative food at low prices.

Something else to keep in mind is that the closer you are to the source of your food, the better it tastes. LA is on the ocean so there is fresh fish. California is the premier producer of fruits and vegetables in the United States and there are so many farms nearby. Of course, there are also cattle ranches and chicken farms
25 to supply the meat.

Los Angeles has become home to one of the most vibrant food cultures in the world by thinking outside the box. LA chefs tried something new by combining food cultures, using mobile restaurants and taking advantage of the fresh local produce. *Bon Appétit!*

Notes steeped in「〜に染まる、没頭する」　Roy Choi「ロイ・チョイ（韓国のテイストを取り入れたタコストラックで一躍有名となった）」　a fraction of「〜のほんの一部」　Bon Appétit!「（フランス語）さあ召し上がれ！」

A Answer if the following statements are true (T) or false (F).

1. Many of the hot chefs in LA have multicultural backgrounds.　　[T / F]

2. Roy Choi started his business selling tacos from a truck.　　[T / F]

3. LA is full of fresh fruits and vegetables, but not locally produced meat.

[T / F]

B Answer the following questions.

1. What kind of tacos did Roy Choi create?

_____

2. How did social media help a lot of chefs in LA?

_____

世界屈指の技術者とクリエイターを育む街

　　日本では「ロス」という愛称で親しまれているロサンゼルス。ディズニーランドやハリウッド、ベニスやサンタモニカの美しいビーチを有し、アメリカ屈指のリゾート都市という印象が強いかもしれません。旅行先として国内外から多くの人が訪れるのはもちろんですが、カリフォルニア州には、国内でも上位に入るカリフォルニア大学ロサンゼルス校（UCLA）やカリフォルニア州立大学（CSU）をはじめとする名門の大学や語学学校も多く、留学先としても人気があります。

　　カリフォルニア工科大学（California Institute of Technology）は、マサチューセッツ工科大学（MIT）と並ぶ全米トップの工学系大学で、卒業生にはIntelやHotmailなどのIT企業の創始者が名を連ねています。カリフォルニア大学ロサンゼルス校（UCLA）は、過去13人のノーベル受賞者を、また南カリフォルニア大学（USC）は、映画監督のジョージ・ルーカスを輩出しています。映画業界を志す学生にとっては、ワーナー・ブラザーズの建物で学べる映画学校のアメリカン・フィルム・インスティティュートや、ウォルト・ディズニー社との関わりの深いカリフォルニア芸術大学など、映画の本場で映画制作や特殊メイクなどの勉強ができることも大きな魅力の1つです。

　　ロサンゼルスは年間を通じて気候が良く、観光にも留学にも、そして散策にももってこいの場所です。ロサンゼルスを訪れたら、日中はビーチやハリウッドを散策し、夜は映画『ラ・ラ・ランド』（2016）にも登場するグリフィス天文台から、街の夜景を楽しんでみませんか。

The Griffith Observatory at night

American Voices #14

If you could stay any age, what age would you stay? Before you watch the video, share your ideas with your partner.

online / video
online / audio
DL 29   CD 29

A Who said it? Match the person with what was said.

1 [   ]   **2** [   ]   **3** [   ]

a. I would stay healthy. Doesn't matter what age I am.

b. To be honest, I'd like to go back to 18 and do some things over again.

c. I don't regret any of it. There are many mistakes that I made, but I don't regret it.

B Watch the video again. Which of the following did John say?

a. I try to compare different periods in my life.

b. I try not to compare different periods in my life.

c. I try to make tomorrow better than today.

C Share your ideas with your classmates.

1. Brian says he enjoys growing old. Will you be happy to grow old? Why or why not?

2. John's counselor said to him, "John, every time in your time should be the best time of your life." Is this the best time in your life?

Listening Highlight

インタビューでは、即答するのが難しい質問に対して様々なつなぎ言葉が使われています。"I'd like to say"や、"That's a hard question to answer"、"kind of"といった表現は、ちょっとした間を埋めることができます。"Oh man"は、「おお」「へーっ」「あらまあ」といった意味で、男女ともに使います。このように、質問に対して少し考える間が欲しい時は、"Well..."「ええと」や"I would say..."「〜かなあ」などの表現を使ってみませんか。

Chapter 15
Seattle, Washington

シアトルと言えば何を思い浮かべますか。その姿形から日本の富士山を思い起こさせるレーニア山は、アメリカ西海岸北西部に位置するワシントン州最大の都市シアトルのシンボルとして知られています。また、コーヒーの街として世界的に有名で、スターバックスやタリーズコーヒーなどの1号店もあります。シアトルは、アマゾン・ドット・コムやマイクロソフト社などの大企業が集まる街でありながら、世界遺産の国立公園や美しいビーチといった豊かな自然に恵まれ、「エメラルド・シティ」の愛称で親しまれています。

Warm-up

Work in pairs and answer the questions.

1. Locate Seattle on the map on page 8.
2. How often and where do you usually buy groceries? Why do you shop there?
3. What is your favorite season and why?

Match each word or phrase with the Japanese.

1. thrift store [   ]
2. epicenter [   ]
3. delicacy [   ]
4. precipitation [   ]

5. moderate [   ]
6. prowess [   ]
7. left wing [   ]
8. liberal [   ]

a. 珍味	**b.** 左派の	**c.** 穏やかにする	**d.** 発信地
e. 優れた能力	**f.** リサイクルショップ	**g.** 自由主義の	**h.** 降水量

Part 1 Getting to Know the Place   online / video

Watch the video and answer the following questions about Seattle.

1 What is true about Pike Place Market?

a. It started in 1909.
b. It gets 15 million visitors a year.
c. It's the 33rd most visited tourist attraction in the world.

2 Something different about the original Starbucks logo was that…

a. it was a man.
b. it was brown.
c. it had less writing.

3 Daniel describes Capitol Hill as…

a. a wild place.
b. very conservative.
c. tightly knit.

4 What does Quinn NOT mention he can buy in the International District?

a. Ramen

b. Manga

c. Video games

Part 2 **Learning More**

(online / video)

Watch the video about the climate of Seattle and what locals think of the city, and then complete the following notes.

Climate = one of the ^{1}_____ cities in the US, but it's seasonal

- *Winter*   The rainiest in ^{2}_____, and very high in
              ^{3}_____ in winter
- *Jun. to Sep.*   The ^{4}_____ precipitation in the US.

▶ *According to a man who moved to Seattle…*

- He realized how unbelievably ^{5}_____ the summers are.
  ➡ Crystal ^{6}_____ skies, no clouds for 60 ^{7}_____ days

- Seattle doesn't get the ^{8}_____ weather.
  ➡ Don't get ^{9}_____ waves or the ^{10}_____ temperatures
    Why?: the weather is ^{11}_____ by the Pacific Ocean,
    the Puget Sound, and Lake Washington.

People in Seattle

- *The vibe of Seattle is…*
  Individualistic prowess, ^{12}_____, ^{13}_____

- He likes to tell Seattleites that they don't ^{14}_____ live in the
  US. ➡ Surprising and ^{15}_____ to them
- The West Coast of the US (Seattle and Portland, etc.) is extraordinarily
  ^{16}_____ and left wing.
  ➡ He's enjoyed being not the ^{17}_____ liberal person.

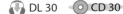

Read the passage and answer the following questions.

Amazon and the Transformation of Seattle

Amazon Seattle headquarters

Seattle has been transformed by big business. In the beginning, it was a logging town. Then came Boeing, and eventually Microsoft. All of these transformed the city in some way, but the
5 arrival of Amazon was something different. In 2007, they announced plans to move into a mostly unused part of downtown called South Lake Union. They would use 11 buildings and predicted they would have 6,000 workers there by the time the campus was
10 finished in 2011. Instead, they employed triple that number of employees.

As you probably know, Amazon just kept expanding. They now employ 50,000 people in the city of Seattle and more than 53,000 when including the surrounding areas. They are the second largest employer in the United States with over 600,000 on the payroll. After the recession in 2008, Seattle had an
15 unemployment rate of 9%, but now it is 3.6%. The city also has one of the highest minimum wages at around $16 per hour.

Of course, people are happy for the higher wages. However, along with that come higher prices and increased population. In the past decade, Seattle's population has increased 19%. This has put a strain on the roads. It is why
20 many people now say traffic is the thing they hate most about living in Seattle. Home prices have also increased as other tech companies such as Facebook and Google have moved in. This is great if you own that home, but not so good if you are looking to buy a house to live in.

Amazon has changed Seattle a great deal since it moved in to those 11
25 buildings. It now occupies a massive space of 37 buildings with plans to expand past 40 in the coming years. They have also planned to build a second headquarters and had an open competition to decide where to put it. How will the second headquarters affect the new city? Only time will tell.

> **Notes**
> Boeing「ボーイング社（シカゴに本社を置く世界最大の航空機メーカー）」　South Lake Union「サウス・レイク・ユニオン（ダウンタウンシアトルとレイク・ユニオンの間の地域で、商業地域と湖が近くにある立地を活かして近年再開発が進んでいる）」　payroll「従業員名簿」　minimum wage「最低賃金」　past「〜を超えて」

A Answer if the following statements are true (T) or false (F).

1. Amazon is the first big company to move into Seattle. [T / F]
2. Amazon is the second largest employer in the United States. [T / F]
3. Amazon has decided to build a second headquarters in Seattle. [T / F]

B Answer the following questions.

1. What are two positive things that Amazon has brought to Seattle?

   _____

2. What happened to Seattle as a result of the increased population?

   _____

発祥は魚市場！動機付けを高める働き方の哲学

　入り口に "Public Market Center" の看板があるパイク・プレイス・マーケットは、1907年に設立されたアメリカで最も歴史のある市場の一つです。迷路のような長いマーケットに所狭しと様々な商品が並べられ、多くの買い物客で賑わっています。

　この市場にある魚屋は、「フィッシュ哲学（Fish! Philosophy）」という経営理論が生まれた場所としても知られています。「フィッシュ哲学」とは、楽しく働きながら生産性を高めることを目指した行動規範で、"Be There"（注意を向ける）、"Play"（遊び心を持つ）、"Make Their Day"（人を喜ばせる）、"Choose Your Attitude"（態度を選ぶ）の４つの原則から成り立っています。さびれた魚市場を活性化しようと導入したのがきっかけとされていますが、今ではお客さんの注文が入ると、店員が氷の上の魚をカウンターのスタッフに投げ、それを見てお客さんが笑う、といった一連のパフォーマンスがとても人気です。日本でも、「フィッシュ哲学」の理論が動機付けを高める手法として医療現場で導入され、成果を上げていると言われています。

　シアトルはスターバックスコーヒーの創業の地でもあります。今では世界的コーヒーチェーンとなったスタバですが、彼らのミッションの１つに「誰もが自分の居場所と感じられるような文化を作る」ことが掲げられています。創業者ハワード・シュルツの言葉の１つ "We are not in the coffee business serving people, but in the people business serving coffee."（我々はコーヒー業界で人にサービスを提供しているのではなく、人間相手のサービス業界にいてコーヒーを提供している）からも感じられるように、商品を超えた付加価値を提供するという姿勢は、パイク・プレイス・マーケットを代表する２つの場所―魚市場とスターバックス―に共通する心意気なのかもしれません。

Pike Place Fish Company

American Voices #15

Let's meet Maddie, a young Seattleite who has grown up in this liberal city.

online/video
online/audio

DL 31   CD 31

A **Watch Maddie's interview and check 3 things that match what she says.**

☐ It is nice to grow up in a place where everyone agrees.

☐ In Seattle, people have different opinions, but they are very inclusive.

☐ She is the president of the feminist club.

☐ Feminism creates equal rights for women and men.

☐ It is not difficult to fight for your rights in Seattle.

B **Which of the following did Maddie NOT mention about her idea of a better world?**

A better world 10 years from now would look like...

a. everyone happy. Us living in harmony, equal rights, equal pay.

b. everyone happy, environmentally sustainable. No war between countries.

c. a happy place where it is safe enough to walk alone at night.

C **Share your ideas with your classmates.**

1. What social issues are you concerned about? How did you become interested in them?

2. If you could change 2-3 things to make your country a better place ten years from now, what would they be?

Listening Highlight

Seattleの [t] の発音は「シアトル」と母音を入れてしまいがちで、難しい発音の1つです。実際のネイティブの発音は、t の音が有声音に挟まれることにより有声化され、「スィアロー」に近い発音になります。Maddie のインタビューからは、彼女はシアトルのリベラルな社会のあり方に賛同していることがうかがえます。"There's no injustice in prisons. There's no injustice in the workplace." といったリフレイン（繰り返し）の使用は演説でもよく用いられる手法で、人々の耳に残る話し方と言えるでしょう。

このテキストのメインページ
www.kinsei-do.co.jp/plusmedia/40

次のページの QR コードを読み取る
直接ページにジャンプできます

オンライン映像配信サービス「plus⁺Media」について

本テキストの映像と音声は plus⁺Media ページ（www.kinsei-do.co.jp/plusmedia）から、ストリーミング再生でご利用いただけます。手順は以下に従ってください。

ログイン

ログインページ

●ご利用には、ログインが必要です。
　サイトのログインページ（www.kinsei-do.co.jp/plusmedia/login）へ行き、plus⁺Media パスワード（次のページのシールをはがしたあとに印字されている数字とアルファベット）を入力します。

●パスワードは各テキストにつき 1 つです。
　有効期限は、<u>はじめてログインした時点から 1 年間</u>になります。

[利用方法]

次のページにある QR コード、もしくは plus⁺Media トップページ（www.kinsei-do.co.jp/plusmedia）から該当するテキストを選んで、そのテキストのメインページにジャンプしてください。

plus+Media トップ　　　　　　メインページ

メニューページ　　　　　　再生画面

「Video」「Audio」をタッチすると、それぞれのメニューページにジャンプしますので、そこから該当する項目を選べば、ストリーミングが開始されます。

[推奨環境]

iOS (iPhone, iPad)	OS: iOS 6 〜 13 ブラウザ：標準ブラウザ	Android	OS: Android 4.x 〜 9.0 ブラウザ：標準ブラウザ、Chrome
PC	OS: Windows 7/8/8.1/10, MacOS X　ブラウザ: Internet Explorer 10/11, Microsoft Edge, Firefox 48以降, Chrome 53以降, Safari		

※最新の推奨環境についてはウェブサイトをご確認ください。
※上記の推奨環境を満たしている場合でも、機種によってはご利用いただけない場合もあります。また、推奨環境は技術動向等により変更される場合があります。予めご了承ください。

本書には CD（別売）があります

American Vibes
People, Places and Perspectives

映像で学ぶアメリカの素顔：都市・人々・視点

2020 年 1 月 20 日　初版第 1 刷発行
2024 年 2 月 20 日　初版第 7 刷発行

著　者　Todd Rucynski
　　　　中 川 洋 子

発行者　福 岡 正 人
発行所　株式会社　金 星 堂

（〒 101-0051）東京都千代田区神田神保町 3-21
Tel. (03) 3263-3828（営業部）
(03) 3263-3997（編集部）
Fax (03) 3263-0716
https://www.kinsei-do.co.jp

編集担当　蔦原美智・西田 碧　　　　　　　Printed in Japan
印刷所・製本所／大日本印刷株式会社

ISBN978-4-7647-4094-5　C1082